Tim Wesemann is a new voice in Christian thought with his heart in the right place—in the very palm of God's hand.

Michael O'Connor,
author of *Sermon on the Mound*

With marvelous stories and his own unique and godly insights Tim Wesemann brings to vibrant life what knowing and loving Christ can mean to those of us who believe.

Gayle Roper,
author of *Spring Rain*
and *Riding the Waves*

Reading *Seasons under the Son* is like reading the private journal of a person who walks and talks with Jesus on a daily basis. The words and message of this book have this amazing depth and richness, kind of like those favorite old hymns, the ones that you sometimes just open up and read aloud because they're so insightful and beautiful.

Rene Gutteridge,
author of *Ghost Writer*

Tim Wesemann's book is a sweet journey through the seasons of faith. Take a quiet moment and enjoy!

Karen Kingsbury,
author of *Moment of Weakness*

Reflections and stories that will touch your heart and expand your spirit. Tim Wesemann's book is a gift for all seasons in life's journey.

James Scott Bell,
author of *City of Angels*
and *Angels Flight*

Seasons under the Son

Stories

Seasons
UNDER THE
Son

TIM WESEMANN

of grace

CPH.
SAINT LOUIS

Copyright © 2002 Tim Wesemann

Published by Concordia Publishing House
3558 S. Jefferson Avenue, St. Louis, MO 63118-3968
Manufactured in the United States of America

Library of Congress Cataloging-in-Publication Data

Wesemann, Tim, 1960–
        Seasons under the Son : stories of grace / Tim Wesemann.
                p. cm.
        ISBN 0-570-05293-9
        1. Meditations. 2. Spiritual life—Lutheran Church—Meditations.
I. Title.
        BV4832.3 .W47 2002
        242—dc21   2001004762

1 2 3 4 5 6 7 8 9 10   11 10 09 08 07 06 05 04 03 02

...to my three seasons of Sonshine:
Benjamin, Sarah, and Christopher

Foreward

*"There is a time for everything, and
a season for every activity under
heaven ..." Ecclesiastes 3:1*

Reflect on the seasons of your life as I consider some of mine:

> ... seasons under the sunshine of laughter, smiles, and joy;
>
> ... seasons under the dark clouds of depression;
>
> ... seasons under the light of hope;
>
> ... seasons under an eclipse of suffering and grief;
>
> ... seasons under the warmth of friends and family;
>
> ... seasons under the cold winds of loneliness;
>
> ... seasons under attack in spiritual warfare;
>
> ... and seasons developed under the fire of faith.

All of these seasons that God has entrusted to my care (and yours) have been lived under an umbrella of the grace of His Son, my Savior and yours, Jesus Christ. There is a time and a season for every activity under the sun. There is also a time and a season for every activity under the Son.

The words that have found their home between the covers of this book are stories of grace—undeserved love. Their purpose is to give God the glory and to draw all who read them into a new or closer relationship with the Son, through the power of the Holy Spirit. The words lead us through the seasons of the life of Jesus and all who follow Him as disciples. Prayerfully and joyfully savor the Savior and His seasons of grace.

+ + + + +

In considering this book, my heart is filled with gratitude for so many people. Some were sent by God to encourage and inspire me in writing it. Some God sent to be a support team for my life. Others have been wonderful prayer partners in my writing ventures. As I acknowledge some here, I realize there are many other "gifts" who aren't mentioned. Special thanks go to:

Chiara, Benjamin, Sarah, and Christopher ... thanks for supporting my writing, putting up with me, and for usually letting me use my computer if I have a creative thought to record, even if you're in the middle of a computer game or it's time for supper;

Linda Rogers for being my "editor-before-'The-Editor'" (I'm glad my typos were entertaining while keeping your wrist and red pen busy marking the pages);

My brothers and sister—Don, Cathy, and Ted for your support in all I do—you mean so much to me;

Don Wesemann, Richard Selzer, Dennis White, and Venice Williams for their beautiful contributions to this work;

Salem Lutheran Church and School in Affton, Missouri, and Zion Lutheran Church in Pevely, Missouri, for supporting my writing ministry and for the honor of serving as your pastor;

Mona Hodgson and the Gorieta Christian Writers' Conference for being a catalyst in my ventures;

Stephen, Agnes, Albert, Renato, Hannelore, Caterina, Phil, the MoWeRS group, Max, Robert, and, and, and ...

And a standing ovation of thanks to CPH for allowing God to share His love through the pages of this book. There is special gratitude within me for my wonderful, encouraging and helpful editors—Jane, Peggy, and Dawn—along with the entire CPH staff who allowed God to use their minds, hands, and talents on this project.

I pray that God will bring out His best in all of us as we journey through the seasons of life under the grace of the Son of God, Jesus Christ.

I would love to hear how God has been working in your life of faith as you read *Seasons under the Son*. Please feel free to contact me at TimWrite@aol.com.

Table of Contents

A Season of Faith and Fire

Epilogue

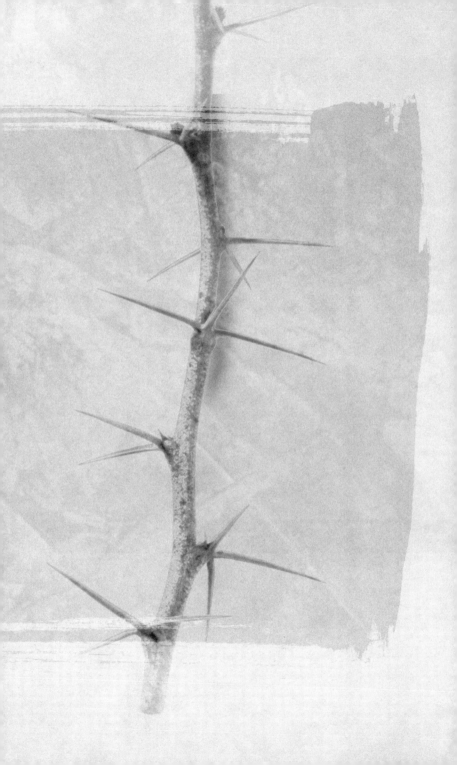

Prepa

A SEASON OF PREPARATION

The Importance of a Stable Environment

Mary and Joseph weren't fully prepared for the journey to Bethlehem. I'm not just referring to their taxing census-taking trip shortly before Mary gave birth, I'm referring also to their entire pilgrimage through the pregnancy months leading to the birth of Jesus in Bethlehem.

Their world shook beneath them with the news that Mary was pregnant. It rocked Joseph's world so violently that he was ready to divorce her quietly. He had the option of divorcing her publicly, which could have led to Mary being stoned. Mary also had to deal with being pregnant during the time of betrothal, a nine- to twelve- month period in which a couple, although deemed married, was not to have a sexual relationship. "Dealing with it" included harassment, rejection, gossip, and probably much worse.

Their stable environment was shaken to the core. They must have longed for stability during that most difficult and confusing time as they prepared for their child—God's child—to be born.

Although we may use other words to describe it, we all long for stability. There is something deeply comforting about a stable environment. All of creation is in a pregnant state, waiting to be delivered from the instability of life on earth as we journey to the new Jerusalem of heaven. Along the way there is harassment, rejection, gossip, and so much more. Often our lives are shaken to the core and we wonder if we will make it.

We could all tell stories of how we weren't prepared for experiences that shook our lives. But allow me to share the story of one "Mary and Joseph" couple who have spent ministry time surrounded by instability. They wrote the following in an Advent/Christmas letter. It needs to be shared.

+ + + + +

"We want to tell you about T. J., who is being raised by his mother, who suffers from schizophrenia. T. J. is a quiet, even-tempered teenager, who is trying to finish school yet has to deal with a drug-addicted brother, who beats up T. J. and their mother every month or so. His girlfriend will be giving birth to their child in a few months. Surely T. J. is one of the faces at the manger this year.

"We are also traveling with Kendall, who told his peers he was a homosexual more than a year ago but is trying to come to terms with what it all means now. His dad is quite ill and his mother has had a nervous breakdown. The school gave Kendall clothes, but he is ashamed of his whole person, his whole life, so he seldom goes to school. On Saturday, my husband will take Kendall for a haircut and conversation. They will talk about Kendall being robbed at gunpoint, and how he was made to strip, and how none of this is his fault. Surely Kendall is anxious for the Christ Child this year.

"Lorna spent the night here last night. She had no change of clothes because her mother sold them all to support her drug addiction. Lorna lives in a crack house—her mother's house—with her younger brother and sisters and whomever else is passing through. Lorna is an extremely quiet girl who watches everything. There are strange, older men hanging out at her house these days. Talking to her. Telling her how pretty she is. Touching her. We are hurrying to get Lorna to the manger.

"Tony is like a son to us. He is with us weekly, often for days at a time. He is one of the lead voices in the Youth Choir and a gifted visual artist. He spends most of his time thinking. Just thinking. Earlier this year, Tony started selling drugs because he and his brothers had nothing to eat when they awakened each morning. He is presently in the ninth grade for a second time and still has less than a 1.0 grade point average on a 4.0 scale. Tony wants to be an architect. Our deal with Tony is this: each time he pulls a grade up, we will enroll him in an art class at a local Art and Design Institute. He starts a drawing class in January and an improvisational composition class in February. Tony arrived at the stable, in advance, found some wood, and built the manger.

"Mario has the potential to be a good student. But he is angry and he doesn't understand his own anger. His attitude prevents him from learning. He was dropped from the eighth-grade basketball team because he failed to get at least a 2.0 grade point average. This past Thursday evening, Mario's aunt brought him to the team's basketball game anyway, just so he could see. Remember. Set some goals. It is a blessing to have Mario's aunt journey to the manger with us.

"There are so many traveling to Bethlehem and who will be at the manger with us. Hoping. Waiting. Expecting this Baby to make things okay in this world. This divine

Baby also wants to use our hands. Our voices. Our compassion.

"I hope you are not traveling to the manger alone this year. I hope there are young people, frail people, poor people, and even strong people journeying with you."

+ + + + +

That letter and message needed to be shared, not only because it tells us of the importance and desire for a stable environment, but because it reminds us where we find stability: in the stable environment named Jesus. The one who turned the insecurities caused by sin into the security of an eternal promise.

In His stable environment, we find the hope and peace we are seeking. We find it nowhere else. Mary and Joseph's world was shaken, but God brought them comfort and truth through His presence and promises. Surrounded by the instability of this unexpected pregnancy, Mary confidently said to the angel, "May it be to me as you have said."

Whether you are surrounded by an inner city, inner turmoil, instability, or insanity, do not allow the confusion of your environment to cause you to miss *this* message: Do not be afraid! Your Lord has important, stabilizing Good News! For to you is born, in the city of David your Savior, who is Christ the Lord. Prepare for the King of stability to come into your heart and life!

The Shepherds Quaked, Shouldn't We?

When I think of earthquakes, California comes to mind. But in 1990, Iben Browning, a scientist from New Mexico, predicted an earthquake along the New Madrid fault. This fault line runs near the Mississippi River in Missouri, beginning in the southeast part of the state. This wasn't a general prediction, but a specific one—the earthquake would occur on or around December 3.

For months many in the area seemed to be obsessed with that prediction, although other scientists said it was impossible to foretell an earthquake. Homeowners ran to look for earthquake insurance. The Red Cross erected emergency shelters. People put together "earthquake kits" and carried them in their cars. Canned foods were hoarded. Everyone spent time preparing for something that didn't happen. December 3, 1990, came and went. The national media packed up, left New Madrid, and went home with the story that there was no story.

In one sense, it was good for the area residents to realize that, before this prediction, they had not made any earthquake preparations. And since they live on a fault line, it is good to be prepared—as prepared as one can be—for an earthquake. Depending on where you live, it is good to be prepared for quakes, tornadoes, hurricanes, and other natural disasters.

It is interesting that the predicted date fell during the first week of December, the beginning of Advent. The word "Advent" means "coming" and it is a season of preparation. It is a time when we prepare for three things: Jesus' coming at Christmas through His birth; the Lord coming to us daily through His Word, Baptism, and the Lord's Supper; and His return one day.

When we consider Christ's coming to the world that first Christmas, we should remember the birth with great awe and wonder. Yet we often miss the awesomeness of the moment because the holiday has become so commercialized. The shepherds who were invited to the Messiah's manger quaked with awe. "An angel of the Lord appeared to [the shepherds], and the glory of the Lord shone around them, and [the shepherds] were terrified. But the angel said to them, 'Do not be afraid. I bring you good news of great joy that will be for all people'" (Luke 2:9–10).

The shepherds quaked, shouldn't we? They quaked with awe at the sights and sounds of the holy night. God sent angels to tell them His message of the Messiah's birth. They quaked with terror and amazement. They took in His presence as they presented their worship at His manger bed. They had reason to quake before the very sight of God and His heavenly hosts.

God came to the shepherds in an astonishing way with an incredible message. It's not so different today. Through words found in His Word, God creates faith and changes lives. The message tells not only of Jesus' birth, but also of His life, death, resurrection, and so much more. It tells not only where Jesus lived while on earth, but that He now comes to live within us. This message of love, forgiveness, and eternal life is awesome. It should leave us quaking in the presence of God. He has chosen to reveal His message to *us!*

The shepherds quaked, shouldn't we? Do you tremble in amazement as you receive the very body and blood of Jesus Christ found in, with, and under the bread and wine? The gift of Jesus Himself is yours. Prepare to quake as He shakes your world with His love.

No matter what time of the year you read this, celebrate Jesus' birth. As you do, prepare to quake at the magnitude of God's gift to you and to the entire world in the form of His Son. Realize the humility of God taking on the very nature of a man. Rejoice in the true meaning of the Gift named Jesus. Prepare daily for His being born anew within your life. And be prepared for His return!

Christ is coming back! This is a certain prediction—a truth to take seriously. It is also a prediction we can look forward to. No, we don't know the date. The Lord will return unexpectedly. No one can foretell it. But by our Spirit-created faith in Him, we don't have to quake in fear of His return. Rather we can again quake with awe at His love in giving us heaven—although we deserve hell. We can quake with excitement about the sure promise of eternal life through that Child who was born to die so we will live!

The shepherds quaked, shouldn't we? Definitely, fellow joy-filled quakers ... definitely!

Quake at His Grace

It was a holy, special night
  Shepherds were quaking at the sight,
  The sight of God's great angel host
  Proclaiming peace to every coast.

The skies were filled with angel flight
  Telling of One who is the Light
  The birth of Jesus Christ their Lord.
  Messiah, Savior, King adored.

The shepherds said, "Let us go see,"
  Can this be true? How can this be?
  And coming to the manger bed
  They worshiped Christ, as they were led.

The shepherds quaked, and shouldn't we?
  Quake at His grace on bended knee.
  Don't quake in fear but rather, awe,
  At all He's said and all you saw.

Quake brothers, sisters, everyone,
  This Savior has our victory won.
  He rocks our world with news of life,
  Forgiveness, strength through ev'ry strife.

God is our refuge and our strength,
  For us He'll go to any length.
  Therefore don't fear though earth gives way
  But quake with those who know The Way.

The shepherds quaked, and shouldn't we?
Quake at His grace on bended knee.
Come watch The Child climb Calv'ry's tree
Then quake some more—He sets you free.

Comfort, Comfort, My People! Amen to That!

The sign on the door read "3523." Beyond the door was a woman who lay dying. Her Advent King seemed ready to carry her home. I was her pastor, and I was there not only to visit but, as the Lord says in the book of Isaiah, I was called to comfort her.

She was uncomfortable with the process of dying and wanted to get on with living—the kind of living that lies beyond death's door. She was uncomfortable being in the hospital and wanted to be in her own bed. She was uncomfortable with her pain.

She was uncomfortable. That fact was evident as she struggled to move her weakened body. It was obvious from our conversation. And it was written all over her face.

Due to her frail condition, I didn't stay long. We visited briefly before heading to the comfort portion of our time together. I opened my Bible to Psalm 46 and read,

"God is our refuge and strength, an ever-present help in trouble. Therefore we will not fear, though the earth give way ... The LORD Almighty is with us; the God of Jacob is our fortress. ... Be still, and know that I am God; ... the LORD Almighty is with us; the God of Jacob is our fortress" (Psalm 46:1–11).

I expounded on the text and attempted to take the words off the page and place them into her troubled heart, like putting salve on an open wound. It was not working. The words of the Gospel salve were flowing, but her soul seemed to reject its healing potential.

Instead she shared her disappointment with God. She cried out with her words and actions about feeling abandoned by her divine Friend as she writhed in pain.

I dipped back into God's Word for more heavenly salve. I wasn't sure that it took. I turned to prayer. And then I closed with the Lord's benediction. Speaking her name, I said, "'The LORD bless you and keep you; the LORD make His face shine upon you and be gracious to you; the LORD turn His face toward you and give you peace" (Numbers 6:24–26).

She beat me to the next word. "Amen," she said. I joined in with my own "Amen."

With that I turned toward the door. With my back to room 3523, I walked down the corridor wondering what went wrong. The Lord had anointed me to bring Good News to the afflicted; He had sent me to bind up the brokenhearted (along with Isaiah and other prophets, pastors, and all Christians called to serve).

Then I met a man who explained her condition; not her doctor but rather the hospital chaplain. As we talked, I realized that I had expected too much of myself. Instead of having faith that God would work through me to apply the healing Gospel salve, I had tried to do it myself. I had forgotten that only God can bring His children closer to Him.

My friend, the chaplain, explained that he had seen many afflicted with the same condition as this woman. He shared that many times he had left a patient feeling as though he had brought them no comfort. He diagnosed this as the affliction of being *un-comfort-able*.

Some days people simply cannot be comforted. They are *un-comfort-able*. God unwrapped this truth for me in the hospital that day.

I had seen evidence of this *un-comfort-able* woman's faith. It had not disappeared. The surgeon had not accidentally removed it. She was just so wrapped up in the pain of her disease and the process of dying that she chose to be *un-comfort-able*. I wondered if she would have been comfortable enough to reach out for Christ's own comfort and healing had He Himself dangled the hem of His garment in front of her.

As I thought about it, I realized I had seen a lot of faithful Christians who were *un-comfort-able*. For some it lasted only a moment, sometimes for one horrific day, while for others it continued for weeks and months. That's when we get comfortable in our *un-comfort-able* state, which can be spiritually (and physically) dangerous. We get so wrapped up in our problems and the accompanying self-pity that we become *un-comfort-able*. This is unfortunate, but it is a reality in a world that is comfortable with sin.

I was perplexed with what had happened in room 3523. On the way home, I realized I had become too wrapped up in the thought that she was *un-comfort-able*. I had been focusing on her pain and discomfort almost as much as she. I remembered the last word she said. It was "Amen." She said Amen to the Lord's benediction that enveloped her life, her condition, her faith walk. Amen means "so be it." God Himself had comforted her, and I almost missed it! The Lord's benediction is not a wish. As it is spoken, the Lord blesses you and He keeps you. He gives you His peace. The Gospel salve had been absorbed because of God's work in her heart, and the *un-comfort-able* wound began to heal.

As I left, I realized that although I had come to minister *to* her, instead I had been ministered to *by* her and our Lord who loved us both. The Lord ministered to me through her with one word of faith. That one word said volumes about our Lord and His for love her and her faithful love for Him. "Amen! So be it, Lord!"

Two days later I received a call from the woman's family. That afternoon the Comforter came in person to room 3523 and made her perfectly comfortable. The Anointed One bound up her broken heart, freed her from the suffering, and brought her to new life. I was more than comfort-able with that news!

And I would not be the least bit surprised if, as our Lord wrapped His loving arms around her and carried her to His gift of heaven, she responded with a hearty "Amen!"

Lord, Quiet Me

Based on Zephaniah 3:17

Lives are crashing all around me,
  Dreams lie shattered like debris.
  I cry aloud to heav'n above,
  "Lord, quiet me with Your love."

The sounds of hatred pierce the night,
  Everyone's wrong—no one's right.
  I cry aloud to heaven above,
  "Lord, quiet me with Your love."

Hearts are racing—tension's high.
  Anger rages, "Why, Lord? Why?"
  I cry aloud to heaven above,
  "Lord, quiet me with Your love."

It's hard to find a quiet place;
  The world is on a deadly pace.
  I cry aloud to heaven above,
  "Lord, quiet me with Your love."

"Lord, quiet me. Lord, quiet me.
  Lord, quiet me with Your love."

The Way in the Manger

(Can be sung to tune: "Away in the Manger")

The Way in a manger, Christ Jesus' His name
Forgiveness He brought us, for sinners He came.
For He is the Way and the Truth and the Life,
And joy He will bring us amidst worldly strife.

The Way in a manger, we give Him our praise
For life so abundant, our voices we raise.
And heav'n will be ours, by faith in the Way;
With joy let us live, for eternal our days.

The Way in a manger, our lives let us give,
For born was this Child to die so we'll live.
Now lead us, dear Jesus, each step of the way
Through life and through death near Your heart
we will stay.

A SEASON OF CELEBRATION

ation

From *The Message*

Celebrate God all day, every day. I mean, *revel* in Him! Make it as clear as you can to all you meet that you're on their side, working with them and not against them. Help them see that the Master is about to arrive. He could show up any minute!

Don't fret or worry. Instead of worrying, pray. Let petitions and praise shape your worries into prayers, letting God know your concerns. Before you know it, a sense of God's wholeness, everything coming together for good, will come and settle you down. It's wonderful what happens when Christ displaces worry at the center of your life.

(adapted from Philippians 4:4–7)

FROM MY THOUGHTS

The trading season is open!
Straight up! One for one! I'll take Christ over worry.
Give me praying over fretting.
And celebrating God all day, every day over anything and everything!

Sitting on His Lap
in the Middle of the Mall

In those days, the calendar issued a decree that all the world should be taxed. And so all went to the mall for a taxing day of Christmas shopping.

And our family also went up to the mall because we belonged to the credit line of MasterCard. I went there to shop with Chiara, my spouse, being great with children (three of them to be precise—and she *is* great with them).

And so it was that, while we were there, the hours were accomplished that presents should be purchased. And we bought forth our first present, had it gift wrapped, and placed it in my hand because there was no room for it in the stroller.

And there were in the middle of the mall parents abiding in a line, keeping watch over their children with might. And lo, the attraction caught their eyes and the excitement of sitting on his lap shone all over their faces; and I was sore afraid.

And my wife said unto me, "Fear not, for behold, I bring you good tidings of great joy: the line is not too long!"

"Not too long?" I protested. "The sign reads, 'Only a three-day wait from this point!'"

"That's three hours, honey, *hours!* You should have seen it last year," my wife responded calmly.

And suddenly there was with my wife a multitude of (okay, there were three) angelic faces, crying and shouting with glee, "Pleeeeeeease, Daddy, pleeeeeease!"

And it came to pass, as the little angels quieted down, that I reluctantly said, "Okay, let us go and stand in line to see this one who bids us come."

The three hours actually went by faster than I thought they would—it seemed more like two hours and 48 minutes. My wife passed the time shopping while I waited with the children. The children passed the time asking me questions like, "How much longer, Dad? Are we almost to the front of the line? Are you going to sit on his lap?"

I was able to conquer all three questions with one answer, "NO!"

The children continued to ask their questions and planned what they would say when they got to the front of the line. The couple in front of us argued over what china they should use when their family came for Christmas dinner. My body was standing in line but my mind was elsewhere. Shivers went up and down my spine as visions of Christmas bills danced in my head. Mentally, I reviewed the "honey, do" list I had received as an early Christmas present back in May. I'd better be checking it twice. Being impatient, I yelled "no, no, no" again and again at my children. My anger brewed at the thought of my wife shopping while I was stuck waiting in line. (I know I said she could shop, but I didn't think she'd take me up on it!)

I thought about my busy schedule and the little time to accomplish it all. I worried about what china pattern the people in front of me would choose for Aunt Nellie. I stewed. I brewed. I stood with a pout as my nerves grew taut. And then my world, which was growing complex, was suddenly shattered by a voice calling, "Next!"

It was our turn! I quickly tucked in shirts and brushed three tousled heads of hair. I wiped the chocolate off the littlest face, and ... hey, where did the chocolate come from? We didn't have any chocolate! There was no time to play detective now. We were next. The crowd was growing impatient!

"Where is he, Dad? I don't see him," the children chimed in.

"He's right through that door," replied a helpful, angelic voice. "Go on in, he will see you now."

Heading toward the door, in true Scroogian style, I mumbled and grumbled about the time we had wasted. I mocked the people falling all over themselves just to get a chance to sit on his lap.

As the door opened, the children let go of my hand and went running to him. They jumped on his lap and threw their arms around him. Their smiles were more animated than I had ever seen. I stood in amazement.

And there he was. Let me re-punctuate that ... and there *H*e was! I had expected a jolly ol' man in a red suit and white beard! I couldn't look Him in the eye. I dropped my packages and fell to the floor.

"Don't be afraid, My child!" I slowly lifted my head to see which one of my children He was talking to. But He was addressing me! "Come, there is room for you!"

"But I'm an adult," I replied, "I couldn't sit on Your lap!"

"Come, My child, come talk to Me." I hesitantly took my place on His lap next to my children.

My oldest spoke first, "Jesus, this year for Christmas I want to tell you about Billy, my friend at school. I've told him about You, and he wants to come to church and Sunday school but his mom won't let him. Will you help his mom understand what it means to talk to You, to worship You, to live for You, and to sit on Your lap?"

Without skipping a beat, my daughter went on and on about a missionary in Togo who was sick, her uncle who lost his job, and a nativity set she made in preschool.

Our littlest told Jesus about his boo-boo, and then he sang a most moving chorus of "Jesus Loves Me."

The tears were streaming down my cheeks when He turned to me. I was next. My mouth went numb. I couldn't speak. But my Lord heard every word my heart had spoken. He looked inside my repentant heart and offered me forgiveness. To my thankfulness He responded, "You're welcome." He recharged my patience, strengthened my faith, adjusted my vision, erased my worries, calmed my fears, and dried my tears.

Jesus was in the mall today! I sat on His lap! He spoke to me! I gave Him all my cares and He cared for me! My heart was racing with such vigor that I ... I ... woke myself up.

I adjusted my eyes to the clock on my nightstand; 4:16 A.M. Christmas Eve. It was all a dream. Sitting on "His" lap in the middle of the mall was all a dream!

But as the clock on the nightstand made its rounds, I reflected on the reality of it all. Jesus *is* in the mall. He is in my house, my office, the kitchen, the car, and at the ball game. He is in my heart. He is in the manger. He is on the cross. He is at the entrance to the empty tomb. He is on the hill where He ascended into heaven, having said, "Lo, I am with you always, even to the end of the age" (Matthew 28:20).

Jesus Christ is coming to town! Jesus is here! Immanuel, God with us is with us! And our world will never be the same.

"Jesus," I prayed, "this is a taxing time. But, Jesus, never let me be too busy, too proud, too taxed, or too embarrassed to jump up in Your lap and throw my arms around You, along with my cares and my praise. And at the same time, Jesus, lead me through Your Spirit to always hold You close in my heart. Good night, Jesus. I enjoyed the visit. Thank You! And Merry Christmas! I hope You enjoy YOUR day! Amen."

+ + + + +

And it came to pass in those days, that there went out a decree from Caesar Augustus, that all the world should be taxed. (And this taxing was first made when Cyrenius was governor of Syria.) And all went to be taxed, every one into his own city. And Joseph also went up from Galilee, out of the city of Nazareth, into Judea, unto the city of David, which is called Bethlehem; (because he was of the house and lineage of David) to be taxed with Mary his espoused wife, being great with child. And so it was, that, while they were there, the days were accomplished that she should be delivered. And she brought forth her firstborn son, and wrapped Him in swaddling clothes, and laid Him in a manger; because there was no room for them in the inn. (Luke 2:1–7 KJV)

Have a Mary Christmas

One day a young girl named Mary is doing chores around her home, and suddenly heaven reveals to her that God will be conceived within her womb. One moment Mary prays with her family that the Messiah would deliver her people. The next moment an angel delivers the message that she will be delivering the very Son of God.

And that was just the beginning. There were longing prayers; the inconceivable announcement of a virgin's miraculous conception; the time trying to get Joseph to understand; the questions and looks from so-called friends and the rumors that followed; the stay with Elizabeth; the morning sickness; the swollen ankles; the emotions—oh, the emotions; the rejection at the inn; the labor pains; the pain; the emotions; the pain ... the pain ... the birth! The tears shared by all!

The tiny fingers! One ... two ... three ... yes, all 10 of them, and toes too! And what now, God? The confusion, the peace that surpassed her understanding, the solitude, the shepherds, the holiness, holding her son—God's Son.

Her little boy was the very Son of God in flesh and bones! The promised Messiah. It was the holiest of nights. And Mary treasured up all these things and pondered them in her heart. How could she not—she was a mother! She was a young teenager of extraordinary faith who knew that this ordinary child was no ordinary child. *She was holding God while God was holding her.*

She treasured and pondered all these things in her heart.

She could have asked for pity. I mean, come on, giving birth where animals give birth? She could have looked for glory ... "Look what I've done!" She could have shooed those unimpressive shepherds back to their fields and told them to send someone with a title in their place. She could have tried to steal the moment from God. But she didn't.

She didn't allow the noise from the streets to pierce the holiness of the moment. She didn't allow the smell of the animals to taint the scent of God's promises that radiated from her son, His Son. She could have done so many things differently. But she didn't.

What she did do was treasure all the events, emotions, thoughts, hopes, and dreams. She pondered them in her heart as she embraced her heaven-sent gift and as her faith embraced the Giver of the most precious of gifts.

She must have also thanked God for keeping His Word while shuddering a bit at the realization. Did she cup her baby's heel in her hand as she recalled God's promise to Eve about the Messiah's heel, which would be bruised as He would one day crush Satan's head?

Did she smile while mentally running through all the "nicknames" the Bible had for her Jesus: Wonderful Counselor, Mighty God, Everlasting Father, Prince of Peace, Emmanuel?

But did her smile vanish for a moment as she wondered about the words of Isaiah regarding the Suffering Servant? The One who would be pierced for our transgressions, cursed for our iniquities, and by whose wounds we would be healed. It's easy to imagine her pulling Him close to her body and kissing His forehead, oblivious to the fact that one day that forehead would be pierced and bloodied from a crown of thorns following a kiss of betrayal.

As she pondered His feet that fit easily in the palm of her hand, she had little idea that these feet would lead millions to heaven. These were feet that would one day walk on water and run off Satan.

When she placed her baby into His manger bed for sleep, did His arms reach outward for her love and affection? These same outstretched hands would one day be nailed to a cross in a gesture of love and affection for the world that nailed Him there.

Mary didn't want to lose a moment. She made a mental scrapbook. She didn't want one emotion to pass without fully experiencing it and thanking God for it. She wanted to bask in the glory and the holiness of the night. So she worshiped with the shepherds, stood in awe with Joseph, and pondered and treasured all the moments that surrounded the birth of Jesus.

Our Lord would have each Christmas be a "Mary" Christmas for us. He wants us to do what Mary did—to treasure and ponder the wonder and glory of it all. God doesn't want us to forget the night when He reached into the deepest cove of His heart, pulled out His love, and laid it in a manger, saying, "For to us a Son is given. ... He will be called Wonderful Counselor, Mighty God, Everlasting Father, the Prince of Peace" (Isaiah 9:6). God sent His only Son to earth, knowing that His blood would be shed and His body given for us, so we could be forgiven.

Savor the Savior and all that surrounds His birth and life! Come to Bethlehem and see this gift of love given for you. Come see heaven's gift of salvation lying in the hay. It is there, under the Christmas tree—a tree in the shape of a cross that looms in the background over the entire scene of glory. Treasure it all. Treasure it today. Treasure it into all your tomorrows.

Treasure and ponder the majesty. The humility. The grace. The strength. The forgiveness. The joy. The emotions. Ponder the peace that surpasses our human understanding. May you have a Mary Christmas overflowing with joy!

I'm Telling

The story of the birth of Christ is a telling one.

God *told* Adam and Eve. The prophets *told* the people. Gabriel *told* Mary. The angel of the Lord *told* Joseph. Mary *told* Elizabeth. Elizabeth *told* Zechariah. Joseph *told* the innkeepers. Angels and their songs *told* the shepherds. The shepherds *told* all they met. The Holy Spirit *told* Simeon. In a land far away, the star *told* the Magi. The Magi *told* Herod. King Herod *told* his teachers of the law. They *told* the Magi. I'm sure the Magi *told* the Easterners. The Bible *told* me, as did my mother, pastors, and Sunday school teachers. I've *told* my children. And now I'm *telling* you!

No doubt about it—the story of Jesus Christ is a telling one. But now that I think about it, how telling *is* it these days? Today it seems to be more of a *listening* story. We have heard the story of Jesus' birth many, many times. But how often have we told it?

Jesus' birth is definitely a story to behold. But it is also a story to be told and retold.

What a privilege it is to tell others the story of the Christ Child, who was born to die but lived to tell about it! Even if you don't have a master's in communications, the Master can communicate through you. He tells His masterfully telling story not only through your words, but also through your Christlike acts of humility, love, and childlike faith.

Who did the Master use to tell His story in the first place? Sinners and saints, angels and archangels, uneducated shepherds and unsuspecting merchants, the rich and the poor, teenagers and teachers, relatives and strangers, His creation and His life-creating Word. Isn't that telling you something wonderful?

God wants you to hear His story. He calls you to join Mary in pondering Your Savior and His story in your heart. He wants you to behold His majesty and marvel at His humility. He wants to tell His story through you and me—forgiven sinners and forever saints, whether rich or poor, uneducated or unsuspecting, teenagers or any-agers, pastors or teachers. All of God's creation needs to know of its Creator. A world of sinners needs to know their Savior. They need to know that Jesus is born, that Jesus died, that He lives, and that He loves them more than anyone else in all creation. All that is told in the story of the birth of Jesus.

I'm telling! How about you?

"The Hopes and Fears of All the Years Are Met in Thee Tonight"

"Mommy! I'm scared!"

Everyone around us in Meramec Caverns heard my shout when they turned out the lights. Total darkness. If you've never experienced it, the little child in me will confirm that it is scary.

Those same words slipped out whenever I woke in the middle of the night from bad dreams. But I wouldn't share the details with my mom because my nightmares usually involved her death, and it was never peaceful, but scary. Since my dad had died some years earlier, I was afraid I would be left alone if my mom died too. Where would I live? An orphanage? Would I move in with relatives? "Mommy, I'm scared, but I can't tell you why!"

A fourth-grade social studies test. I slowly turned over the graded test Mrs. Fahrenbrink placed on my desk. I peeked with one eye, squinting, as though that might help. It didn't. It was much worse than I imagined. I had failed. A big fat F was marked on the top of my test. I had never failed a test before. I'd have to tell my mom. But how could I? Could I keep it from her? I was afraid. I spent much of my day trying to figure out how to tell her, or *if* I should tell her. I found out later that I had wasted a lot of time worrying. My mom was a teacher at the same school, and she had known about my grade since noon when she had eaten lunch with Mrs. Fahrenbrink. She was also interested in knowing how or if I was going to tell her.

"Mommy, I'm afraid!"

... of that strange man with the red suit and white beard who had an extremely deep voice and limited vocabulary!

... of the way Jesus looked at me from the big cross in church. He looked so disappointed, almost mad. Did He really love me? *Could* He love me?

... of mean, loud people; of being lost in a store; of doing something so bad my family wouldn't forgive me or love me anymore; of monster Halloween masks; and of hell and sometimes even thoughts of heaven that I didn't understand.

I can't remember what I wore last Tuesday, what I ate for supper two Fridays ago, or the last five movies I've seen. But I remember those fears from my life that are almost 40 years old.

Neither can I remember what I hoped to get for Christmas last year or what I hoped to have for supper a couple of Fridays ago.

However, I remember I used to hope that one day I'd have a family just like the Brady Bunch and that I would be the Peter Brady of the family. (That would be so far out and groovy!) I hoped that when I grew up, I would marry Florence Henderson and have six children and a dog named Tiger. Shirley Jones would have been okay too if Florence wasn't available.

I spent time daydreaming about being a pitcher for the St. Louis Cardinals. Oh, how I hoped and longed for that to become reality. If not, I hoped to be a teacher or pastor.

I hoped that my mom would never die and that they would never cancel the Brady Bunch. I looked forward to meeting my dad and my grandpa in heaven, since they died just months before I was born and I never got to meet them and they never had the opportunity to hold me.

I looked forward to being able to take Communion with all the big people ... wondering about the mystery of it all.

+ + + + +

We've all had plenty of hopeful moments and enough fears to keep us shaking a while. Surely your fears and hopes are easy to recall.

Have you ever been afraid that God's love is conditional after all? Be honest. Have you ever wondered if God will really forgive *all* your sins—even that secret one you're trying to hide from Him and everyone else? Afraid you'll grow old alone and end up in an old house surrounded by 19 old cats? Are you afraid of dying? Afraid of living? Are you fearful that your children will feel like strangers when they are grown or even when they are teenagers? Are you afraid the past will catch up with you or the future fail you?

What about your hopes? Do you hope for a day when finances aren't a burden? Hoping the dream bubble doesn't burst on your dream home (or is it more like a dream mansion)? Hoping forgiveness is for giving and not just talking about? Dreaming of a love so fulfilling you'll never feel lonely, hurt, or empty again? Hoping and waiting for a baby to be born?

Dear little, unassuming Bethlehem: "the hopes and fears of all the years are met in thee tonight."

Bethlehem? God sent Micah to tell His people that out of the little town of Bethlehem someone great would come. He would be a ruler. He was there in the beginning, as God, who created the world. Yet He would find a beginning in a bed of hay surrounded by a young maiden, a carpenter, and some shepherds.

For in this Bethlehem bed laid One who would transform the hopes and fears of all the years. Your fears and mine. My hopes and your dreams. In this Bethlehem-born Child, the hopes and fears of all the years would meet.

In the eye of this tempestuous mixture of both hopes and fears, comes—as I view it—a kind of divine explosion. He destroyed the reality of our fears, leaving each of us with a new life filled with eternal hope in Him. The manger Messiah came to fill the dangerously deep, dark valleys of fear for you. And He makes your mountain peak dreams align with His.

Fear not! The darkness of your cavernous life is over; the Light has returned. Don't be afraid! The Light of the World has invaded your world. You won't be left in the dark again.

Whether you've seen an F on a test or feel like you're wearing one on your forehead from failing life, realize this: Jesus was born to die. He was born to die for you and me! And in His death, He took all of our failures with Him to the tomb. They are buried, never to be seen or heard from again.

But *He* will be seen again! In His miraculous resurrection, Jesus raises us to new heights of living—victoriously, abundantly, forgiven, and eternally.

With His graceful presence, Jesus takes our hopes and shapes them for us. Through Him we have a sure and certain hope in matters of faith and hope-filled dreams of learning to be content in all circumstances. Our dream houses turn into the mansions in heaven. Our hope for forgiveness is cemented below us as an unmovable foundation. Our financial concerns are leveled by the fact that the baby boy named Jesus lived out the meaning of His name, Savior, as He paid our debt of sin. God puts His Spirit in our hearts as a deposit, guaranteeing what is to come—the glorious return of Christ (2 Corinthians 1:22b).

It all comes together in Bethlehem. The hopes and fears of all the years are met in Bethlehem's most important citizen, Jesus Christ, who has taken up residence in our lives.

"Fear not: for, behold, I bring you good tidings of great joy, which shall be to all people. For unto you is born this day in the city of David a Savior, which is Christ the Lord. And this shall be a sign unto you: You shall find the babe wrapped in swaddling clothes, lying in a manger. ... The shepherds said one to another, Let us now go even unto Bethlehem, and see this thing which is come to pass, which the Lord has made known to us" (Luke 2:10–15 KJV). And they came with haste (without fear and with high hopes, I'm certain), and they found Mary and Joseph, and Bethlehem's baby—your Savior, my Savior, the world's Savior—who was lying in a manger.

"... the hopes and fears of all the years are met in thee tonight" (from "O Little Town of Bethlehem").

A New Year's "Eve"

Only a week after Christmas and the lights on the tree seem dim. The tree is more of a fire hazard than a remembrance of the season. The ornaments will soon be history. And the eggnog is beginning to curdle. It must be a new year!

A new year can be a time for lists, resolutions, and beginnings. If that is your prayer as you pour out the eggnog, vacuum the pine needles, and continue to thank God for His gift of Jesus, then God has some ideas and encouragement for you. In fact, God invites you to celebrate a new year any day of the year!

Here's the plan: Begin in the beginning. Grab your Bible and read the first new year's day account—in the beginning—paying particular attention to Eve. The news is found in Genesis 1:1–5:5 and the story of a new year's Eve.

1. *Be a helper* (Genesis 2:18). Eve was called a helper to Adam. Look for ways you can be God's helper, seeking to share His love with others. Rejoice that God is your ever-present help in time of need.

2. *Work on your listening skills* (Genesis 2:1–17). Adam told Eve that God had forbidden them to eat the fruit of the tree of knowledge. She may have heard, but she didn't truly listen. Listen to God's Law as it guides you in the Lord's ways, and listen attentively to His Gospel that offers forgiveness and hope for all our days and ways.

3. *Desire wisdom* (Genesis 3:6). What a wise gift! Pray that God will help you discern His ways from Satan's deceptions.

4. *Watch what you sink your teeth into* (Genesis 3:6). Sink your teeth into God-pleasing projects. He wants to use you as His hands and feet in this world. Be careful not to choose projects for your own glory. (We're back to number three!)

5. *Live in God's promises* (Genesis 3:15). Immediately after sin entered the world, God promised Eve (and the world) a Savior. Celebrate that promise as you live daily as a forgiven sinner.

6. *Raise a little "Cain"* (Genesis 4:1). Take a stand for God and His ways. Raise a little "Cain" in a godly way! (He'll make sure you're "Abel." Sorry, I couldn't resist!)

7. *Mourn, but not like those without hope* (Genesis 4:8). Because of sin, difficult news will come every year. Eve grieved the loss of her son, but even in her grief, she hoped in God's promise of a Savior. Know there is always hope through Jesus Christ, no matter what.

8. *Seek God's plan for your life* (Genesis 5:4). God's plan for Eve was to be a faithful wife and mother. Seek God's vocation for your life. Rejoice in His plan and follow it faithfully and gracefully by the power of the Holy Spirit.

9. *Take a "peace" of paradise with you into every day* (Genesis 3:23–24). Like Eve, we know what it is like to live outside of paradise. Also like Eve, we take a "peace" of paradise with us as God comes to us. And He does come to us through His Word and the vehicles of His grace, empowering us to live in His presence and promises. One day, by God's grace and sacrifice, we will know perfect peace in His eternal paradise.

10. *Have a happy new year's "Eve," whatever day it is!*

A SEASON OF LIGHTS

The Light over the Water

This is an epiphany story. A story of lights. A story of visitors from the east. A story of sea turtles.

My family traveled eastward to the South Carolina coast. One bright sunny day, we happened upon a nest of sea turtle eggs in the sand dunes. Through a local, who was watching over the eggs while their "parents" were off at sea, God taught us about His creation and kingdom.

Each summer along certain areas of the eastern coast, female sea turtles make a trek from the ocean to the shore to lay their eggs in the dunes. This trip is usually made at night, most often when there is a full moon. After the eggs are laid, the mother returns to the sea.

About two months later, something remarkable happens. As the eggs hatch, little sea turtles pop out from the shells. Off they run down the beach, straight for the ocean, soon to be lost from human sight in the waves.

How do they know which way to run? God has created an instinct within them to recognize and head for the water lit by the reflection of the moon and stars. Running toward the light over the water, they dive into their life as sea turtles.

But there is one concern. Many beaches where these turtles nest are becoming overcrowded with houses and businesses. With these buildings come many artificial lights—lights that confuse little sea turtles, lights that may lead them astray and to their death. Many turtles are found dead on roads because they headed toward artificial lights rather than God's lights placed over the ocean.

Sea turtles ... Magi. Both are often in the dark when it comes to following lights.

In the East, there lived a group of Magi who began a journey westward. They knew to go west because the Creator designed a star in the sky to lead them to a place in Bethlehem. As they drew near, they sought the help of the local king, Herod, to find a child known as the king of the Jews. After receiving direction from his own wise men, King Herod told the Magi to return to him after they found the child so he could also worship the new king.

The Magi made this trek to worship. They came and laid their gifts before the one named Jesus. They had seen *His* star. God's light had shone on them and led them.

They could have easily made a deadly mistake en route. For while the Magi were worshiping Jesus, Satan was hard at work in the heart of King Herod, planning to kill the Christ Child. Herod was afraid that this child would take his earthly throne. His declaration that he would like to worship the child king served as a false light, beckoning the Magi to return to the deceitful king's palace. But the true Light of the world warned the Magi in a dream not to go back to Herod. Recognizing the true Light, the Magi were led by God's illuminating grace.

Sea turtles ... you and me. We are often in the dark when it comes to following lights.

Every day we awake and pop out from under the cotton shells that blanket us. And off we go running into the new day the Lord has created and entrusted to our care. But how do we know which way to run?

That can be a problem. Satan is hard at work filling our day with artificial lights—people glowing with deceit, events that blind us, false truths and hopes that blur our vision, words that light roads that are dead ends. These lights bewilder us. They can lead us astray and sometimes to death. Satan is very good at making artificial lights appear real. It can be quite confusing at times.

But God through His Word has given His children knowledge of the Light of World—the promised Messiah, our Savior, Jesus Christ. He has told us that Jesus is the *only* way to salvation. He calls, "Come follow Me and I will give you life—abundant, forgiven, and eternal."

There is one way to be sure you are being led by the true Light that leads to life. As you head into each day, move toward the Light that is over the water. As fast as your faith can take you, run for the Light reflected on the water of Baptism. Satan doesn't play in that water. That's where you will find safety; that is where you will find your new life.

Tomorrow, as you break out of your cotton shell, reflect on the story of the Light over the water. Then dive gracefully into another day in God's kingdom of light!

A Different Route Home

I once received an e-mail retelling the Epiphany story.
It was titled "If Wise Women Had Visited the Christ Child
instead of Wise Men." I didn't save it, but I remember one
thought: "The Wise Women would have stopped to ask for
directions so they would have been on time, and they
would have brought more practical gifts like diapers,
pacifiers, and a casserole."

Then I received an e-mail with a response to this story
as found in "Dear Abby": The Wise Men *did* stop to ask
for directions—from King Herod. Because they stopped to
ask about the baby king, Herod ordered all the boys two
years and younger in Bethlehem and its vicinity to be
killed. Someone else wrote similar thoughts and ended
with "Little wonder that men have been afraid to ask for
directions ever since!"

Jokes and stories about the lack of a male direction
gene have been around for years. Some take it all the way
back to Moses, who led the Israelites around the wilderness for 40 years. ("If he had only stopped for directions,
they would have reached the Promised Land much soon-
er!") Personally, I don't have a problem asking for directions. Problems arise as I attempt to follow them.

We often remember the Wise Men's journey to
Bethlehem but overlook a very important part—their trip
home. With all the exciting elements of their westward
excursion—the star, the meeting with King Herod, the joy
in their arrival, their time of worship, and their gifts—it is
easy to gloss over the fact that "having been warned in a

dream not to go back to Herod, they returned to their country by another route" (Matthew 2:12).

Herod told the Wise Men to return after finding the child known as king of the Jews. Herod said he wanted to know where the baby was so he could go and worship him too. We know that was the *last* thing he wanted to do. Insanely jealous, Herod would do anything to destroy a rival king. The Magi were warned of this and instructed to go home by a different route.

God safely directed the Wise Men to worship the divine Child by providing a star to follow. Then He charted their safe course home. To me, this is much more than a geographic course of travel. It is the dream-come-true gospel of what God wants for each of us when we spend time with Jesus in worship. He leads us to return home, to our daily lives, by a different route. This new route to life is charted in the perfect presence of the King of the Jews and Gentiles—the King of the world—Jesus Christ. In His perfection, we realize our imperfections. The light of His Word leads us to forgiveness, repentance, and a complete change in our walk through life. We no longer walk alone on the paths we have blindly treaded in sin. Instead, we are carried by Christ on the heavenly path of grace.

It's intriguing for me to imagine the homeward conversation of the Gentile Wise Men. It's also interesting to wonder if their spiritual journey followed a new and different route. Did they leave their reverence for eastern gods lying on the road outside Bethlehem after revering the One who would remove their sins "as far as the East is from the West"? Did they, like the shepherds, spread the word concerning Him while returning home, glorifying and praising God for all they saw and heard?

The Bible doesn't give us these answers. But it does give us directions. We can find God, the Father, only through Jesus Christ, God the Son. Jesus said, "I am the Way and the Truth and the Life. No one comes to the Father except through Me" (John 14:6).

The Bible is the map to the Christ Child, and it lights the way through this life to our perfect life in heaven (Psalm 119:105). As Jesus comes to us and we respond to His love in worship—praising, praying, and confessing—we are changed, empowered, and forgiven by the power of God's Word and the tangible evidence of His grace through bread and wine. All who have been baptized into Christ's life-changing love return home by a different route (2 Corinthians 2:17).

The next time you're driving home from work, school, or another familiar place, take a different route home. Not only is it a good way to get out of a rut, but let it also remind you of the new route home the Lord has revealed to you. Wise men, women, and children—let's look for one another on the new road home while spreading the Good News of our life-changing Savior to the rest of the world!

From *The Message*

We pray that you'll have the strength to stick it out over the long haul—not the grim strength of gritting your teeth but the glory-strength God gives. It is strength that endures the unendurable and spills over into joy, thanking the Father who makes us strong enough to take part in everything bright and beautiful that He has for us. (adapted from Colossians 1:11–13)

From My Thoughts

Lord, I'm gritting and grinding my teeth. I don't want to just get by. I desire your glory-strength! I want to race past the enemy with passion, joy, and thanksgiving! Amen.

Only the Best

The mood was one of joy and celebration. Music filled the air. People traded stories. There was dancing and laughter. The people were filled with joy. It was a wedding feast!

It was a good day. There was food. There was wine ... well, there *was* wine! It was almost gone and with it would go the dignity of the host. Mary, Jesus' mother, came to Him with the message that people would soon be thirsty.

Appropriately enough, at the wedding Jesus brought gifts. To His disciples He gave an epiphany gift—a manifestation of who He was. To the wedding couple and their families, He gave a miraculous gift packaged in vessels used for cleansing. It was the gift of wine, needed immediately to quench the thirst of the wedding guests. But this was not just any wine. This was very good wine ... the best. Only the best would do. It was a good day. It was a time to celebrate!

Contrast that scene with a day where the mood was somber. A chorus of lightning and thunder echoed throughout the heavens. People traded stories, and some even traded articles of clothing. There were tears and wailing. Yet we also call this day "good." On this Friday, Jesus came to the people with a request. "I thirst," He said, gasping for breath as He hung by nails.

How did the people respond? As we still do so often— by bringing Jesus much less than the best. Again, a vessel stands near Jesus—a jar full of sour wine. Those near Him put a sponge soaked with the wine on a hyssop stick and held it to His mouth. Some say it was to help with the pain, but did these executioners really care about His pain? No matter, a vinegar-soaked sponge was not the best. Yet God miraculously turned this bad day into His Friday, a good Friday. He brought out His best in His last days— His ultimate gifts to the world: forgiveness, salvation, life, victory. The best of the best. God gave the gift of Himself to a world watered down with sin; a world that so often gives much, much less than its best for Him.

Think of those days in light of our day. Today is a day to celebrate because this is a day the Lord has made! Outwardly we may celebrate, yet inwardly many of us have feelings of emptiness, concern, guilt, worry, and watered-down commitments. Amidst our whining, moaning, and inward groaning, Jesus hears us say, "Savior, we thirst!"

And Jesus comes bearing gifts because He brings a wedding feast to us. It is a foretaste of the eternal feast to come. He hears our thirsty cries and responds with gifts. He brings miraculous gifts wrapped in grace with bows of truth and peace. With His hands of mercy Jesus writes our names on gift tags and calls us to remember that His first miracle with the water and wine was not His last with those same elements, even in these last days. With vessels for cleansing filled with water, Jesus *gifts* us with faith, forgiveness, and eternal life through Baptism. He miraculously changes us from being enemies of God to friends with God. He gives sight to each of us born spiritually blind. He raises each of us from spiritual death to new life in Him.

But the giving doesn't stop there. Although His enemies raised wine vinegar to His lips, Jesus raises a cup of salvation to ours, His forgiven enemies. It is His best. It is His own blood shed for us. He says, "Drink … all of you. This is my blood of the covenant, which is poured out for many for the forgiveness of sins" (Matthew 26:27–28).

His best is now ours. Full, free forgiveness along with a promise that He remembers our sins no more. Jesus gives us perfect love and strength, even when we seem weakest. He also empowers those who have received His best to bring *living water* into a world that is crying out, "We thirst!"

Celebrating the best of this day, we go out as His vessels, filled and overflowing with His grace. We carry the best of God's gifts to others who need to know that with Jesus Christ they shall thirst no more. What a manifestation—an epiphany—of God's best! And through His gifts, He brings out His best in us as we travel through this day of celebrating until we arrive at the heavenly wedding banquet that has no end!

St. Groundhog's Day

Okay, okay, I know Groundhog Day isn't on the church calendar, but there is a lot to learn from the legendary story of Punxsutawney Phil from Pennsylvania. Just in case someone reading this is from another country and is not familiar with Groundhog Day, let's quickly review.

German and British immigrants brought this custom to America as a way to forecast the weather. According to legend, the groundhog wakes from its winter hibernation on February 2, sticks its head out of its home in the ground, and looks around. If the sun is shining, the groundhog, frightened of its shadow, crawls back into its hole. This is supposed to mean there will be six more weeks of winter weather. If the day is cloudy, without shadows, the groundhog stays out of its hole and spring weather is on its way.

Certainly this isn't a scientific method of weather forecasting. Yet on February 2, the media converges on Punxsutawney, Pennsylvania, with cameras, video cameras, and notepads waiting to see if Phil will see his shadow. Poor Phil! Imagine waking up, stretching, and opening your eyes to find a wall of reporters crowding around you, snapping pictures, videotaping, and staring. I'd head back into my den in no time! At that point, my shadow would be the least of my worries.

Are you bombarded with people crowding around you, wanting this and that? Do you wonder if you can keep up with their constant demands? Do you feel like the walls are closing in? Maybe popularity frightens you. Maybe it's the opposite and you feel as though people don't care about anything you do. Perhaps you struggle with living in the shadow of a brother, sister, or friend, and you want your own identity. You may be able to relate to some of the things Punxsutawney Phil deals with each year.

A shadow, or lack of one, plays a major part in observing St. Groundhog's Day ... excuse me, Groundhog Day. Shadows can also play a major role in all of our days. How do you feel about shadows? If you are in a scary situation, an unexpected shadow can bring fear. But shadows can also be a place of relief and rest.

Where I live, the summers can be very hot and humid. My children are involved with baseball and soccer teams. The fields on which they usually play have only a couple of trees along the sidelines. It's humorous to see how many parents try to pack their lawn chairs under the shadow of those trees. As the game wears on and the shadow moves, so do the chairs. The spectators want to take in the temporary relief the shadow brings.

Some might use the shadow of a groundhog to forecast six weeks of weather, but what if we could use a shadow to forecast eternity? This forecast doesn't involve scientific method either. It involves a spiritual truth. The writer of Psalm 91 shares, "He who dwells in the shelter of the Most High will rest in the shadow of the Almighty. I will say of the LORD, 'He is my refuge and my fortress, my God, in whom I trust'" (Psalm 91:1–2). Rest—a true, lasting, refreshing rest—is found in the shadow of the Almighty God.

When Satan turns up the heat in your life, check to see if you're living and resting in the shadow of the cross.

When you feel as though the walls are closing in, find true relief in the shadow of the Lord, a refuge and fortress that cannot be defeated. When everything seems to converge on you, run to the shelter of the Most High and His shadow of rest.

When you poke your head into a new day, notice the shadow of Christ's cross covering you. Don't be afraid of this shadow. It's a refuge for rest, refreshment, and rejoicing. As you live in the shadow of Christ's cross, you can be reminded that no matter what the weather is like for the next six weeks, you have an eternity of restful living in the shadow of the Son!

A SEASON OF SACRIFICES

All I Want

(Based on Philippians 3:10)

All I want …
  All I want …
  Is to know Christ.
  All I want …
  Is to know Christ and experience
  the power of His resurrection;
  To share in His suffering and
  become like Him in death.

That's all I want because Christ changes everything.
  The power of His resurrection changed my life.
  Because He lives, I too shall live eternally.
  There's power in His blood and resurrected body.

All I want …
  All I want …
  Is to know Christ.
  All I want …
  Is to know Christ and experience
  the power of His resurrection;
  To share in His suffering and
  become like Him in death.

His tomb of death was changed into a place of life.
  He came to life to roll away my heart of stone;
  Once I was trapped in cold tombs of self-centeredness,
  Now I share His life and suffering—that's all I want.

All I want ...
  All I want ...
  Is to know Christ.
  All I want ...
  Is to know Christ and experience
  the power of His resurrection;
  To share in His suffering and
  become like Him in death.

Love in the Nursing Home

I wasn't expecting anything out of the ordinary when I left the church office with my surplus of comforting tracts, private Communion set, and pocket Bible. (I've wondered if they make that size Bible for convenience or because it's easy to hide. Unfortunately, I think the answer is sometimes both.) I was off for an afternoon of shut-in and sick calls.

I was saving the best for last ... although I didn't know it at the time. My last stop that day was at a nursing home where two of our church members make their residence. These two are dear, sweet Christians, but there is something about the home that makes me somewhat queasy. I haven't put my finger on it, but as soon as I walk through the front door all of my senses are on alert. I know what you're thinking—the odor. Well, it's more than that. I truly can't explain it, but I would be lying if I said I was not affected.

As I entered the first room, a stranger greeted me with, "You must be Pastor Wesemann." (I guess the pocket Bible gave me away—I was glad it wasn't hidden!) The greeting came from our member's new roommate, whom I had never met. On her lap she had a copy of our church's newsletter turned to an article I had written about loneliness. (I realized the Lord was already there, having placed it in her hands.) I thoroughly enjoyed the visit with both ladies; the joy seemed to drown out the feeling of queasiness that had accompanied me.

As we talked, another resident entered the room, and I had the opportunity to witness what I thought was long lost—the sensitive art of wooing. With a little bend at the waist, he offered both ladies a single violet he had picked in the patio garden. Then he turned to the roommate and asked if she would like to accompany him to the TV room for a viewing of "Newhart." She politely thanked him but declined his offer. He exited with the charm of a refined chap, outwardly gracious in defeat, but I thought I noticed a little dark spot—an inward bruise to his male ego.

Love in the nursing home. How lovely, I thought. A gentleman caring for his lady friends.

In the next moment, the roommate held up the newsletter and shared that she often reads to our shut-in member because her eyes aren't what they used to be.

Love in the nursing home. How lovely, I thought. Roommates sharing more than a room.

As I was sharing the Lord's Supper with the lady I was visiting, somewhere between the Creed and the Lord's Prayer, I glanced across the bed. Mrs. Roommate was reading the article on loneliness. I hoped it would strike a chord in her life.

I continued with, "Take eat ... Take drink. This is the true body and blood of your Savior, poured out on Calvary's cross in love for you, for the forgiveness of all your sins."

Love in the nursing home. How lovely, I thought. A Savior giving His all for His children, breaking down the walls of loneliness with His Word on one side of the room and His body and blood on the other, given and shed for them—a strong reminder that He is their ever-present

Love. This wasn't just a hunch ... the love came to life in her tear-stained cheeks and in the emotional "thank you" that followed.

As I headed to the door, a voice broke the silence, "Are there others from church who will visit?" I said I hoped there would be. "Please come back soon!" I turned to leave and silently asked the Ultimate Lover in the nursing home to remain. He lovingly obliged.

The story could have ended there, but God wanted my cup to overflow, as it did with the next visit. Not only did our Savior remain with the ladies, He accompanied me to another room.

I entered a very plain room, void of many signs of personal life ... no pictures on the walls, no flowers or cards on the dresser. There was artificial life emitting from a radio blaring Dolly Parton's latest. Signs of life were coming from the bed. Trying to keep up with the country tune was a pair of dueling snorers, one of whom I would awaken with the call of his name and a touch on his shoulder. I almost hated to break up their back-up band.

As he woke, I noted that his teeth were taking a rest by the sink and his razor was on vacation. My sense of smell went from Red Alert to Under Fire as I found myself perched over a half-filled jug of urine hanging on the bed rail. I slid it down to the limit of the rail. It didn't help very much. The music still blared. The person across the hall was moaning from obvious pain. The man in the next bed was snoring. And the one I was visiting was filled with cancer.

After a brief visit, I prepared the Lord's Supper. I realized there was no desk or table on which to place the

Communion set. It didn't fit on my lap since my Communion agenda book and pocket Bible had taken up residence there. Making sure no one noticed, I placed the set on the floor. I felt uneasy about it. I don't know why, but I did.

I proceeded. And during the mini-service my guilt was erased and God's grace took over. I had distributed Holy Communion hundreds of times, but this time was different.

I had floored God's means of grace, and He floored me with His grace!

There I was, almost overcome by the smell of urine, the ugliness of sickness, the stench of death, the groans of pain, the cries of loneliness, the noise of artificial life, and the results of sin. I was in the middle of it all ... a part of it and active in it. And there, on the floor, was my Lord's body and blood.

Love in the nursing home. *More than lovely,* I thought. Appropriate! Amazing! Aware of the surroundings. Present because of the surroundings.

Was Christ offended because I assigned Him to the floor? I don't think so. That's where His Father assigned Him—to the floor of the world. Imagine Him there on Golgotha, the "place of the skull." Jesus smelled of sweat and probably urine (as uneasy as that thought may make us). Those around Him cried out in pain. The ground was spotted with broken bones and blood aged in the sun. The observers were stained with sin. The music of heaven played a disturbing chorus of thunder booms and lightning clashes. Total loneliness made Christ's heart throb with pain. The stench of death was right under His nose. He didn't flinch. But He did die.

Love on the floor of the world, thriving amidst death. Love in forgiveness won, blood shed, and sacrifices complete. Love for God's children making their home amid the stench of sin in the trenches of death. Love had come to life on the floor of a nursing home in a way I'd never experienced before.

God saved the best for last that day. He introduced me to a world of love in the nursing home. And what a lovely experience it was!

Sitting on God's Hands

I was surprised when I read a phrase in the Bible that made me laugh. I laughed because of the wording of Mark 10:37 in the New King James Version. James and John came to Jesus with a request: "Grant us that we may sit, one on Your right hand and the other on Your left, in glory."

Maybe it's just me, but that's an amusing mental picture. It sounds as though the disciples wanted to actually "sit" on Jesus' hands in the glory of God's heaven.

Obviously, literally "sitting on Jesus' hands" is not what the text says. But by wanting special positions of glory in heaven, figuratively that's what they were doing. While Jesus was teaching humility and servanthood, the disciples were looking for prestige and power. In a way, they were trying to hold down His hands so they might be lifted up.

John and James brought this request to Jesus as they traveled to Jerusalem. Jesus had just told His disciples about His upcoming suffering, death, and resurrection. During those events, Jesus would use His hands in miraculous ways: to wash the disciples' feet, to eat the Passover meal and institute a new covenant in His blood, to miraculously heal the ear of a soldier in the Garden of Gethsemane. Finally, He allowed His hands to be nailed to a cross.

The same day the world's sin nailed the hands of Jesus to the cross, two other men were executed there—one at His right hand and the other at His left. It wasn't James and John who were crucified at His right and left; it was two criminals. And to one of those, Jesus said, "I tell you the truth, today you will be with Me in paradise" (Luke 23:43). Glory in heaven's paradise would come to a common criminal.

Where were James and John at that moment? Many of the disciples had fled when Jesus was taken away to be tried. John was nearby, but he wasn't at Jesus' right hand or left. He was at the feet of His Savior. He had a close-up view of Jesus' feet, nailed to the cross and covered with sores and blood mixed with dust from walking the "Way of Sorrows."

From his position, John easily heard Jesus calling for him to serve, to care for His mother, Mary. And Jesus told Mary to consider John as her son from that moment on. Although the idea of serving seemed to be lost along the way to Jerusalem, Jesus washed the feet of James, John, and the other disciples, leaving them an example to serve others. And now, even at His death, Jesus taught others to serve as death was being served to Him on a wooden platter in the shape of a cross.

It's easy to desire prestige and power. We like to be recognized and to think we are in control. We want to do the work—even God's work—and get the credit. Do we sit on God's hands? Sometimes we try.

Where would we be without God's hands that formed man from the ground, that held back the waters of the Red Sea, that buried Moses on the mountain, that wrote messages on walls? What could we do without His hands that touched deaf ears so they could hear His name and hope-filled message; hands that blessed bread, fish, and children; hands that wiped away the tears of others as well as His own; and hands that were nailed down and three days later rolled away a boulder that covered His grave of death, turning it into a place of life.

Where would we be without Him? We wouldn't have hands or hand-outs, hand-me-downs or handfuls of blessings. Without our glorious God, we wouldn't be handy with tools or handily win games.

If Roman nails couldn't hold down Jesus' hands, do you think we can? All power, glory, and majesty belong to our Servant King, Jesus. His hands were pierced for our transgressions so He could raise our hands in victory and use our hands in His service.

Having Christ's victory motivates us to allow Him the use of our hands in service. In other words, when it comes to faith, we can't sit on our hands. As we join John and Mary at the foot of the cross, we hear Him say to us, "There is your mother who needs your compassion. There is your son, in need of a family. There is a woman who needs a word of My comfort through your voice. There is a man whose soul is lost ... bring Him to Me. There is a child who needs to know he is important ... in your eyes and Mine. There is ..." The list is unending. God wants to use us. As we head to the new Jerusalem of heaven and all its glory, there isn't time to sit on our hands or His.

Shouldn't we daily be giving Him a hand in thankful service ... more than just a hand, a standing ovation! To God be all glory ... forever and ever!

Final Words and Lasting Moments

(A Song for Maundy Thursday)

(Words written to be sung with the hymn tune:
"Jesus, Refuge of the Weary")

> *Final words and lasting moments;*
> *Bread and body—wine and blood.*
>
> *Bonds are strengthened—one is broken;*
> *Friends forgiv'n while one betrays.*
>
> *In the upper room they gather,*
> *Jesus and the twelve remain,*
>
> *For the hours are quickly moving*
> *toward His death on Calv'ry's tree.*
>
> *Water bowl for dusty trav'lers;*
> *Master teaches how to serve.*
>
> *Words of life and words of comfort*
> *for the dozen who seem dazed.*
>
> *"Never shall You wash me, Savior,"*
> *Peter says, with bold intent.*
>
> *But to live within God's kingdom,*
> *you must humbly learn to serve.*
>
> *While they eat the meal, rememb'ring,*
> *Jesus takes the bread and speaks.*

"This, My body, given for you—
Eat this and remember Me."

Then the cup He lifts toward heaven,
"Drink My blood that's shed for you."

Grace on grace all sin erases, while He
aids their faith to serve.

Thoughts and hymns, reclining com-
ments, they prepare to leave the room.

"Watch and pray, lest you be tempted,
While I go o'er there to pray."

But they slept while Jesus suffered,
praying that God's will be done.

Then the crowd came, led by Judas to
betray Him with a kiss.

Friends of Jesus, come together.
Let us join them, as we learn,

Of that holy Thursday evening where
Christ shares His final words.

Teach us Lord, our gracious Master,
how to serve and to obey,

As Your cross looms in the distance,
may we die and live with You.

A Twisted Love

Sometimes I wonder how some people can become calloused toward their jobs. Is an abortionist really cold to the reality of what he or she is doing? Are the folks who give the fatal injections or hit the switch on the electric chairs affected by what they are paid to do? Do judges wonder if they made the right decisions? Does opening a body with a scalpel become routine for surgeons? Do counselors daydream during sessions? How could the Roman soldiers make a sport of crucifixions?

A sport of crucifixions? I don't understand that, yet the ones overseeing Jesus' execution seemed cold and callous to it all. I realize, of course, that they were just doing their job. It was on the day's agenda, so they did it.

A crucifixion is one of the most, if not *the* most, horrible forms of execution. It was inhumane to drive spikes through hands and feet and force them to bear the weight of the body. The pain was excruciating. Breathing was difficult. It usually took hours for death to come. And the public was invited to watch.

Do you remember the first time you were invited to come to the crucifixion of Jesus? It probably made a lasting impact. Come again with me; we're going right to the foot of the cross.

It's difficult to look Jesus in the eyes or to look at the blood—some still flowing slowly from His forehead, hands, and feet; some caked on His body where it dried in the heat of the sun. From this position, His gasps for breath are overwhelming at times. You want to help Him breathe, don't you? You also want to attack the soldiers for making fun of Him when He appears so helpless. But there is nothing you can do. At the foot of the cross, all your senses work overtime and your emotions are on overload. It's hard not to fall on your knees. You are witnessing not only death, but also love. It is unconditional, sacrificial love that changes and impacts our lives each day.

So why is it often easy for us to walk past the cross of Jesus Christ and not be moved? Have you been there so often that it doesn't seem to really matter? The blood doesn't bother us anymore. The noise of our lives drowns out His words, and His struggle to breathe is hardly noticeable. We have found it easier to move past if we don't get too close. Then the crowd doesn't get in our way.

If you are finding yourself becoming like the soldiers—unaffected, maybe even calloused, by the crucifixion of Jesus Christ—then consider this: Satan is working overtime in your life. Some things should impact us no matter how often we experience them. This is one of them. Set down your calendar, laptop, cell phone, games, and general busy-ness, and come back to the spot Jesus has saved for you. It's right at the foot of the cross. He wants you to witness His love for you through His sacrificial death. He wants you to hear His words of forgiveness, compassion, and commitment, along with His words of both humanity and divinity. Never grow complacent with your daily trips to the cross of Christ.

The willing sacrifice of Jesus Christ is the most beautiful and profound love story ever witnessed or read. It has changed my life. I discovered the second most beautiful love story in an odd place. It was in a book by a surgeon as a reflection on his life and work. The book is *Mortal Lessons—Notes on the Art of Surgery* by Dr. Richard Selzer. He beautifully tells of an experience after performing surgery:

"I stand by the bed where a young woman lies, her face postoperative, her mouth twisted in palsy, clownish. A tiny twig of the facial nerve, the one to the muscles of her mouth, has been severed. She will be thus from now on. The surgeon had followed with religious fervor the curve of her flesh; I promise you that. Nevertheless, to remove the tumor in her cheek, I had cut the little nerve.

"Her young husband is in the room. He stands on the opposite side of the bed, and together they seem to dwell in the evening lamplight, isolated from me, private. Who are they, I ask myself, he and this wry-mouth I have made, who gaze at and touch each other so generously, greedily? The young woman speaks.

"'Will my mouth always be like this?' she asks.

"'Yes,' I say, 'it will. It is because the nerve was cut.'

"She nods, and is silent. But the young man smiles.

"'I like it,' he says. 'It is kind of cute.'

"... Unmindful, he bends to kiss her crooked mouth, and I am so close I can see how he twists his own lips to accommodate hers, to show her that their kiss still works ... I hold my breath and let the wonder in."

From the cross, Jesus mindfully bends to kiss us with His life of love. He twists His own perfect life in pain and agony to accommodate our lives that have become twisted from the deadly imperfection of sin. He does this to show us that His kiss still works. *Hold your breath and let the wonder in.*

His twisted body. The blood flowing. The sacrifice for sinners. *Hold your breath and let the wonder in.*

Forgiveness. Salvation for the world. Taking upon Himself the Father's wrath we deserve because of our sins. *Hold your breath and let the wonder in.*

The cries of pain. The last words that became lasting words. *Hold your breath and let the wonder in.*

He allowed His body to be twisted with pain for us. That's how much He loves us. No matter what, His kiss of love will always work. *Hold your breath and let the wonder in.* Let the life-changing truth of His love in.

An Undivided Heart

(A Prayer of Confession and Forgiveness
based on Psalm 86, especially verse 11)

*Teach me your way, O Lord, and I will walk in your
truth. I am praying for an undivided heart. I desire
for You to take total control of my heart—my life-
being. You have come to rule over all aspects of my
life. I want to trust You with every part of my life.
But so often I find that my heart is divided. The sins
that are a part of my heart break Your heart, Savior.
Hear the private confession of my divided heart ...
(Take time to confess your personal sins)*

*Now Savior, I trust the truth of Your Word which tells
me that when I confess and repent of my sins, You forgive and remember them no more. You have brought
healing to my heart that was divided. You have made
me whole again through Your life, death, and resurrection.*

*You are forgiving and good, O Lord, abounding in love.
Teach me Your way and help me to walk in Your
truth with a heart that is not divided, as I stand in
awe of Your presence in my life.*

*Continue to grant me a heart that is undivided as You
live within me. In Jesus' name, whose heart stopped
beating one Friday afternoon on a cross so my heart
could be healed today and eternally. Amen.*

A Toast to Friends

I've witnessed many toasts at wedding receptions, anniversary parties, and other celebrations. Toasting never meant all that much to me until I attended a wedding reception where the best man explained how the practice began. Centuries ago, many alcoholic beverages were made through a process that involved lead tubing or pipes. As the drink was processed, particles of lead ended up in the drink. These lead particles could cause illness or even death to those who drank them.

As a sign of caring, a host would offer each guest a small piece of toast to place in their drinks. The bread would absorb the foreign, potentially deadly lead particles. Once removed, guests could drink in celebration. To give someone a toast was a sign of love and loyalty.

The night before He was crucified, Jesus lifted a cup to His friends. In essence, He said, "I toast you, My friends. Take eat. Take drink. This is My body and blood shed for you for the forgiveness of all your sins."

On the cross, Jesus absorbed all of our poisonous, deadly sins into His body. His Father did not remove the cup of suffering from His life, rather He caused His Son to raise the cup in a toast like no other—to give His life for us. In return, the Father gave us forgiveness, life, and peace. In raising the cup of salvation, Jesus raises us to new heights as His honored, forgiven brothers and sisters.

I've never looked at toasting in the same way since learning its history. And I've never looked at the Bread of Life in the same way since learning His story. Can you?

The cup has been raised. The toast has been made. The sacrifice is complete.

Looking over His Shoulder

Constantly looking over your shoulder is not good for back, neck, or shoulder muscles. But that doesn't stop most people from spending a lot of time doing so. Fear does that to people. Maybe you're doing it right now. A look here. A glance there. Maybe you're doing it without even realizing it. You've become so used to living in fear, you don't even know you're doing it.

So much time is spent looking over our shoulder for ...
- bill collectors.
- footsteps of guilt from sin that keep a steady beat, following your every move.
- people after your job.
- test scores that will do you in.
- lab reports that follow you out of your doctor's office.
- people out to damage your reputation.

So much time is spent looking over our shoulder because of ...
- fear disguised as lack of confidence.
- fear caused by lack of knowledge.
- fear living with a faith that is weak or dying.
- fear found in living or in dying.
- fear discovered in news that reports drive-by shootings, robberies, assaults, rape, and any other story that can fit in a newscast or on the pages of a newspaper.

Spending time looking over our shoulders in fear caus-es our physical, emotional, mental, and spiritual muscles to ache. If you're in that kind of pain, a remedy is available. The treatment still includes looking over a shoulder—but not your own!

Consider another view, one that has a great advantage. It replaces your fears with confidence and strength.

Look over a different shoulder, one that is drooping a bit. It hangs like that because it belongs to someone who is hanging from a cross. That's right, look over the shoulder of Jesus as He is crucified. His sacrificial act on the cross makes an amazing difference in your life as you are called to carry your cross and follow Him.

As you look over Jesus' shoulder, you can't miss seeing the blood or smelling the sweat caused from carrying the cross in the heat of the sun. You won't miss hearing every gasp for breath as He attempts to push up on the nails that pierce His feet, striving to fill His lungs with air. From this angle, you won't miss His words of forgiveness—words that chase away the sin and guilt that have been chasing you. Neither will you miss Jesus speak with compassion about life and commitment.

From your cross-eyed, over-the-shoulder view, you will witness the darkness that covers the land. And in that darkness, you notice that the One being crucified is lighting the way to salvation for a dying world.

From the cross, looking over Jesus' shoulder, you get a Savior's-eye view of the world. You see people who are standing near the cross and people who are going on with life without even stopping to look up. You see how Jesus is calling all of them to come to His cross of life.

From such a viewpoint, you notice Jesus running off the armies of Satan even as He is nailed to a tree. While hanging there, He crushes the power of our greatest enemies whom we once feared. Although pain racks His body, Jesus is in the process of taking the sting out of death for all who would believe in Him.

Relax your back, neck, and shoulder muscles. Stop looking over *your* shoulder. Start looking over *His* shoulder. You will see that your Savior fearlessly faces death so you can confidently and victoriously face life.

The "I'ves" of March (or any Month)

Dear Father in heaven,

I've had a difficult day . . .

I've been hurtful and hateful . . .

I've had a tough time dealing with those around me . . .

I've lost my patience with my family and friends . . .

I've been uncommitted in following in Your footsteps . . .

I've habits that are hard to break . . .

I've been through the wringer and put others through it by my lack of compassion . . .

I've been keeping so much inside, bottling it up . . .

I've been finding lots of excuses to run away from it all . . .

I've been in a rut . . .

I've lost my zest for life . . .

I've realized I need help . . .

I've missed you.

Signed, Your Child

Dear Child, whom I love,

I've missed you, too!

I've been waiting to hear from you because I have good news!

I've got the answers to all your questions and problems.

I've been watching you, crying for you, wanting to hold you; yet when I come near, you push Me away.

I've always loved you and always will—don't shut Me out.
I've always loved your family. Follow My example as you lead and love them.
I've the forgiveness you need for your hateful and hurtful ways, for your lack of commitment and patience.
I've what it takes to pull you out of your ruts and to put zest, zip, and zeal back into your days.
I've realized you need My help. I want you to know I never left. I want to help!
I've made an eternal commitment to you.
I've sent My only Son, Jesus Christ, to die in your place. That is how much I love you!
I've made sure that He took all your sins and the punishment you deserved on Himself, so you have hope and forgiveness as you live for Me.
I've given you a reason for living, and I have great plans for you!
I've missed you! Come, make yourself at home! You are always welcome here!

With love, your heavenly Father

First published in *Lessons in Dadhood* by Tim Wesemann ©1997, published by Concordia Publishing House.

Resolved

(Based on Luke 9:51)

He set His face on Jerusalem.
Resolved, head up, and confident,
He took the road that led to hell,
So I could go to heaven.
I'm called to follow in His steps.
Resolved, I'll walk His ways.
So Jesus, shine Your face on me,
And lead me to Your cross.

His hand was set upon the plow.
Resolved, He would not turn around,
Except for times I fell behind,
He'd stop to lift me up.
I'm called to follow in His steps.
Resolved, I'll walk His ways.
So Jesus, shine Your face on me,
And lead me to Your cross.

For me, He went to Calvary's cross,
Resolved to die so I could live—
Forgiven and eternally—
My life is surely His.
I'm called to follow in His steps.
Resolved, I'll walk His ways.
So Jesus, shine Your face on me,
And lead me to Your cross.

Jesus, Remember Me

It wasn't a stab in the dark—the thief on a cross on Calvary who said, "Jesus, remember me when You come into Your kingdom" (Luke 23:42).

He probably couldn't explain what exactly was going on within him. He might even have started the day hurling mocking insults at Jesus along with so many others in the crowd. Or maybe he took it all in, observing the faithful followers of Jesus. Whatever happened in the hours or minutes before he spoke to Jesus, one thing is certain: The Holy Spirit created saving faith in this criminal's heart, helping him realize that Jesus had done nothing to deserve death. He cried out to Jesus for salvation. And with all the grace of a dying Savior, Jesus assured him, "I tell you the truth, today you will be with Me in paradise" (Luke 23:43).

What is more remarkable? That the dying criminal used his last words and energy to ask Jesus for a lasting gift or that Jesus granted it? Both are extraordinary, but that is what Jesus is all about. There is nothing ordinary about Him! He calls us to come to Him, led by His Spirit, and gives salvation to all who do. The man was a common criminal. We don't know what he stole. But we know Jesus stole his heart and carried away his sin.

If the nails hadn't been holding the man to that tree, I imagine that he would have fallen on his face at Jesus' feet. Despite His pain, despite the hell He knew was ahead, Jesus gave this criminal a peace he had never before experienced. And in that moment the man received a little bit of paradise. While fastened to the cross-shaped tree, the thief was also grafted to his Savior—as a branch is to a vine. He was nailed to one cross while his sin was nailed to another. He deserved the death sentence but he received a gracious life sentence. Heaven was his—that very day.

There were more miracles on the day Jesus was crucified than we might at first realize. He didn't just die for the salvation of all those in the future who would put their faith in Him. In His last moments on earth, Jesus immediately gave everlasting life to someone many may think was undeserving of such a gift. That sounds exactly like the story of our own encounters with Jesus. It sounds like the story of everyone who has ever lived.

The thief said, "Remember me." Remember that Jesus has remembered you. He remembers your need for a Savior. He remembers the Holy Spirit creating saving faith within you. Never forget that He remembers His daily and eternal promises for your life. Remember that paradise is yours by grace, through faith in the One who hangs around sinners.

From *The Message*

In simple humility, let our gardener, God, landscape you with the Word, making a salvation-garden of your life.

(adapted from James 1:21)

FROM MY THOUGHTS

Dear Gardener:

1. Prune.
2. Chop weeds.
3. Fertilize.
4. Water from the life-giving stream.
5. Landscape with Your creative, artistic touch.

Your work is appreciated! See You at home!

Love, Me

Dear Me:

About your salvation garden: It is finished!

Love, your Gardener

Washed in the Blood of Jesus

*Washed in the blood of Jesus—
    forgiven, cleansed, and free;
    For me, through pain and suffering,
    He died on Calv'ry's tree.
    I give my life to Jesus,
    who lives so I will live;
    Renewed in mind and spirit,
    my all to Him I give.*

*It is my true desire
    to daily keep in mind
    The things of God, most holy—
    my will with God's aligned.
    I walk in Jesus' footsteps,
    I trust where He will lead;
    Abundant life He gives me,
    and meets my every need.*

*His hands and feet were wounded,
    scarred by the Roman nail.
    His cross serves as a bridge now,
    His footsteps lead the trail
    With all the saints together,
    we follow hand in hand,
    Till one day we'll reach heaven—
    The promised glory land.*

Come fill our minds, dear Savior,
with gifts from heav'n above;
When sinful thoughts come tempting,
replace them with Your love.
From fear and worry lead us,
to think on holy things
Receive our prayers and praises,
brought forth on angel's wings.

Opening the Gift of the Magi

Mary knelt on the dirt floor in front of the wooden chest. She slowly ran her hand over the top of it as her fingers outlined a special etching in the wood. Etched in Mary's mind was the memory of her Joseph making the chest as a gift to her in honor of the love they shared. He put such time and devotion into making sure it was his best work. The same hand that explored the trunk moved to wipe a tear that ran down her cheek and settled on her upper lip. She felt the pressure of more tears forming in her eyes, and she buried her face in both hands, sobbing. Mary collapsed onto the ground, her tears dropping like rain falling on a dusty road. The air was filled with her wailing.

"Joseph! My Joseph!" she cried. Hardly a moment passed before she cried out again. "Jesus! My Jesus!" The words mixed with her sobs. But her heart wasn't finished. Looking heavenward, she borrowed words she heard her son speak the previous afternoon, "My God! My God! Why have You forsaken me?" For the next hour, Mary cried, remembered, and wondered.

The Sabbath sun was about to set. It was about this time yesterday when she and Mary Magdalene followed Joseph of Arimathea and Nicodemus as they carefully but quickly wrapped her son's lifeless body in strips of linen. With emotion, they prepared Jesus' body for the tomb. Amid her grief, she found time to appreciate the generosity of this secret follower of Jesus who gave her use of his garden tomb. Mary thought there was something special about her Jesus being buried in the grave owned by a man who had the same name as her husband, Joseph.

The men laid Jesus' body on the stone bed of death. Blood from His hands, feet, and side seeped through the strips of linen. With reverence, they covered His body completely with a large sheet, a shroud. Nicodemus brought a large amount of myrrh mixed with aloe—about a hundred litrai worth—to prepare the body for the sleep of death, according to Jewish custom. But the sun was beginning to set. The Sabbath was closing in. There was no time to properly prepare His body.

With all their might, the men rolled a large stone against the entrance of the tomb before heading home. As they hurried home before sundown, they met Pilate's guards—sent to seal the tomb and stand guard for at least three days—for the chief priests remembered Jesus' words that after three days He would rise.

Mary became aware that, with God's help, she had survived one day after living through the most horrific event of her life. She could hardly bear the sight of her son experiencing such pain and suffering while she was so help-less. She could do nothing. It was a mother's nightmare. She didn't sleep during the night after Jesus' death. Every time she closed her eyes, she saw the gruesome acts of the soldiers. The ringing of the nails pounded into the wood, through her son's hands and feet, echoed in her mind.

Mary absolutely hated her feeling of helplessness. Couldn't the soldiers have allowed her to climb up and wipe the blood and sweat from His eyes that had run down His forehead, pierced from the crown of thorns? She wanted to hold Him; sing Him a psalm of peace; whisper a mother's love in His ear. It was not possible, but she wanted to dream.

"Dear God, my God. Have You forsaken us all?" Mary asked aloud. No one but God heard her question.

All these thoughts brought Mary to tears again. How often would she, could she, relive the execution of her firstborn son, Jesus? Mary rested her head on the wooden chest in front of her. As she did, she remembered why she was kneeling there. She straightened slowly and took a deep breath, trying to compose herself.

She took hold of the latch on the chest and smiled; smiles were rare for her these days. She cradled the latch in her hand for a moment and recalled the day the latch broke and Joseph had to replace it. Joseph had loved to surprise Mary with gifts. On that day, Joseph teased that he had hidden a gift where she wouldn't find it.

After searching here and there for some time, Mary spotted the wooden chest. "It's in there, isn't it, Joseph?" Mary asked with the merriment of a young girl. Joseph just smiled and shared a look that gave his secret away. Both ran to the chest, and Joseph tried to keep Mary from opening it. In the struggle, filled with hilarity, they fell against the chest and broke the latch. They fell backward in a pile of laughter.

The memory found Mary awash with quiet laughter— the kind that comes when a person enjoys the moment but has no one with whom to share the joy. "I miss you and need you, Joseph." Mary said. This time she whispered as though it were a secret she was sharing with herself.

Mary slowly lifted the latch and raised the top of the chest. It was filled with memories. Her emotions worked overtime as she gazed upon the contents. She gently laid her hands atop one of Joseph's robes before lifting it out of the chest and laying it on the floor next to her.

Reaching in again, Mary pulled out a bowl that was some 30 years old and hadn't been used in years. They had purchased it in Egypt, when Jesus was just a little boy, where they hid from Herod and his death threats. A smile crossed her face again as she saw the portion of a torn fishing net Simon Peter once gave her so she would never forget "the best fisherman in the area." (Mary also remembered how long it took her to get the smell of fish out of the net so she could include it in her memory chest.) There was a set of beautiful cups the parents of a wedding couple gave her in gratitude for a miracle Jesus performed at their daughter's marriage feast when they ran out of wine. Then Mary pulled out a covering that her relative, Elizabeth, had made especially for her. Mary pulled it close to her heart. So many memories covered her as she wrapped herself in the blanket made with love. As she set it aside, she saw the reason for rummaging through this chest of memories.

She couldn't bring herself to pick it up just yet. She stared, examining it with her eyes and memory. It was beautiful. Ornate. Expensive. Royal. Mary allowed her mind to travel back to Bethlehem. What a night! Someone had knocked on the door. Shock filled the house, maybe amazement is a better word to describe the moment. A caravan of camels, servants, and Magi filled the street. Mary was speechless, yet without being told, she knew why they were there.

"We have come to worship the One who has been born King of the Jews," they said. Without a word, Joseph held the door open and the Wise Men entered. When they saw the Child King, the Magi bowed down and worshiped Him. Mary remembered that she did what she was best at—she treasured the moment and kept it in her heart. She didn't want to forget any detail.

Mary blinked the memory away and returned her thoughts to the present. Her eyes were still fixed on the inside of the chest. For there, once hidden under Elizabeth's handmade cover, was one of the gifts of the Magi. Joseph and Mary had needed the gift of the Magi's gold to survive their travels to and from Egypt. With gratitude, they had used the Gentile's gift of incense in their years of worship as a family and as a community. How many of their prayers were lifted up to heaven along with the incense given as a gift to Jesus!

One of the Magi's gifts remained. With mixed emotions, she lifted it out of the chest. It was an exquisitely shaped and decorated container filled with myrrh. It could have been viewed as an odd baby gift, for myrrh was a type of resin used in preparing a body for burial. But Mary had kept it all these years. She had always known there was a reason and time for the each of gifts from the Wise Men, and they both belonged to God.

Now, Mary knew, the time and reason for this gift had come at last. Early tomorrow morning she would join other women on a return trip to Jesus' tomb. Nicodemus had already brought a large amount of myrrh to use in anointing Jesus' body in preparation for death. Nevertheless, she must add the myrrh from the Magi. It was prepared especially for Jesus. Mary was certain that her heavenly Father had ordained it.

She lay back down on the floor, clutching the container and wishing she were embracing her son. She knew this myrrh was given to Jesus at His birth to be used at His death. Her tear ducts seemed empty. Exhausted from lack of sleep and emotional turmoil, Mary started to fade off to sleep right there on the floor.

"Joseph! My Joseph!" Mary said softly. "Jesus! My Jesus!" Mary repeated until her words were hardly audible. "God! My God! You have not forsaken me! The gift of myrrh ..." she whispered. "The Magi gave it in worship ... at His birth. My Jesus. He truly was a child born to die. Tomorrow I will anoint His body." Her eyes were closed, she was near sleep. But her voice could faintly be heard, "... my child ... no, His Child ... born to die."

Mary, Mary Quite Contrary

Those who live as Easter people can easily envision Mary Magdalene crying as she stands outside the garden tomb where Jesus was buried. However, one often misses the stark contrasts of the scene. We draw our eyes to Mary's tears but don't see the background. We see the woman but often, like Mary herself, we miss the Man standing there. While noting the tomb of death, we miss the tree of life looming in the distance.

It's a fascinating portrait, "Mary, Mary quite contrary."

Mary Magdalene was a woman possessed. Possessed by what? The answer depends on when you meet her, for timing is everything.

If you meet her before she met Jesus, she was a woman possessed by seven demons, as the inspired writer Luke tells. But she experienced the miracle of life in One from Nazareth. In a word, possibly a touch, or maybe as He called her by name, the demons were removed and replaced with a peace never before known. She saw the One who was Lord, and her life changed. In stark contrast to her former ways, her life now had meaning and purpose. Now she was possessed with the Spirit of the living God.

The Gospel writers tell us that Mary traveled with Jesus, along with the disciples and other recipients of His miracles. She spent her days listening to and learning from her Teacher as her faith bloomed and grew through His words and life. She committed her life to the Lord, who had given her new life. She joined other women, not only following Jesus, but also serving Him and caring for His needs as He went from town to town, sharing the kingdom of God. How else could she have responded? Mary Magdalene had been through Satan's hell and was graciously handed heaven and all its riches by Jesus Christ. How else could she respond to the Giver of such gifts but with a life totally committed to Him? She gave her life to the One who gave her new life.

I hope the picture is starting to come into focus. This is not just Mary's picture—it is every Christian's picture. At first, Mary's situation may appear a bit more dramatic than ours. But is it really? Our picture is not much different from hers. The Bible paints a vivid scene: we were enemies of God, apart from God, blind to His way. "Mary, Mary quite contrary" ... that's how our story goes!

God's grace in calling us by name is no less dramatic and no less real. The contrast is just as startling. The love of our saving God is just as intimate. And the Gospel that calls us to respond is just as powerful.

Daily, we join Mary in the journey to Calvary and the garden tomb owned by Joseph of Arimathea. What a joy to relive the miracle and witness the love! It reminds us of our first time there witnessing the events of God's plan of salvation.

On Mary's journey to Calvary, Scripture tells us she stood at a distance. We can relate to that. It seems safer to hold the cross at a distance. But in doing so, we hold our nail-scarred Savior at a distance as well. And we miss so much. His words of forgiveness are easily drowned out by the strong sound of distracting thunder. Even His final words of victory are muffled by the cries and insults of the crowd.

The empty cross may be in the background in the picture of Easter morning—but it is in the center. It draws us into the scene, causes us to take our eyes off Mary's tears and focus our attention on the cross and the living man/God it once held.

In the garden, Mary focused on her own sorrow. Her tears were real. She was grieving. But in her grief, she almost missed the miracle of life for a second time. Desperate, grieving, and remembering, Mary stood in a puddle of her tears, outside the tomb—not in it. She had already spent time in a tomb of death while possessed by Satan and his demons.

But Mary Magdalene was a woman now possessed by God. She had been called by name and given new life in Christ. As she stood outside His tomb, He called her by name again. The miracle of life would be repeated. Rather than standing at a distance from the cross, she now would want to hold on to her Savior for dear life.

The picture paints a contrast—just like Mary's life.

Her contrary lifestyle would see only hopelessness and despair while her new life basked in the glory of a sure and certain hope through God's presence and promises.

The former life would see only reasons to cry tears of sadness while her new life saw the One who would eternally wipe every tear from her eyes.

The ear of one living apart from Christ hears many distracting voices. How contrary this is to those whom God has called by name. They know the voice of their living Shepherd and they follow Him.

The stories are more similar than we might like to admit, Mary's and ours. For once we lived in darkness amid the tears of hopelessness. But in Baptism we were buried with Christ and raised to new life. There the living Lord called us by name and said, "You are mine ... forever." What a contrast!

Oh, Mary, Mary, quite contrary; how your faith, while in the garden, grows ... for you have seen the Lord. What a beautiful portrait of a woman possessed ... possessed by the living God!

From *The Message*

[Jesus said] "Are you tired? Worn out? ...
Come to Me. Get away with Me and you'll recover
your life. I'll show you how to take a real rest.
Walk with Me and work with Me—watch how I
do it. Learn the unforced rhythms of grace. I
won't lay anything heavy or ill-fitting on you.
Keep company with Me and you'll learn to live
freely and lightly."

(adapted from Matthew 11:28–30)

FROM MY THOUGHTS

The unforced rhythms of grace.
  The unforced rhythms of grace.
    The unforced rhythms of grace.

The company you keep does make a difference!

      The unforced rhythms of grace.
  The unforced rhythms of grace.
The unforced rhythms of grace.

Between a Rock and a Hard Place

One Sunday, a group of women found themselves caught between a rock and a hard place. The "rock" was a large stone rolled in front of a tomb. The "hard place" was the realization that they wouldn't be able to move it and anoint the body inside.

They hadn't given the stone barrier a thought until on their way to the garden tomb. Instead, their minds were on the events of the past three days. Their heads ached from crying and lack of sleep. They walked into the dawning sun, focused on one thing. It was their grief, not their legs, that carried them down the rough walkway. Then suddenly, the women had a reality check. "Who will roll the stone away?" They realized they were between a rock and a hard place.

I've spent time in that place. Have you? It's not comfortable. The rock is any barrier—real or imagined—in front of us. The hard place is worry about the barrier. I've lost sleep, wasted time, ruined moods, and frayed nerves over things like this.

I once saw a greeting card that read "Someday you'll look back on this and wonder why you worried." What a great card to have sent to the women who went to Jesus' tomb. But Scripture doesn't tell us if they were simply concerned or truly worried. There is a difference. There is nothing wrong with concern, but when we cross over the line and begin to worry, we are no longer trusting God. Then we have to deal with another barrier—our sin.

Are you starting to think about the rocks and hard places in your life? Do you recognize your personal barriers and the worry accompanying them? I wonder how much time we have spent worrying about something only to learn it was a complete waste of time. God had already arrived at the scene and taken care of the anticipated problem before we even recognized it.

That's what happened at daybreak that morning. The women who went to the tomb hadn't given a thought as to who would roll the stone away. They also hadn't given a thought to the words of Jesus, telling them He would rise victorious over death.

While the women spent time worrying about the rock, Jesus had already taken care of the hard place. There was no cause for concern. Jesus was alive—just as He promised! Although the rock was on a roll, the women still would not let their blues roll away. Now they were afraid that His body had been stolen. But that had also been taken care of; the Lord provided an angel to tell them He had risen.

Jesus was a step ahead of the women that morning. He also goes ahead of us. Everything that comes into our lives has already passed through the knowledge of God. He has promised that we can listen to, find strength in, and trust in Him. There are so many times we worry about things only to find that Jesus has already taken care of the potential problem.

It's easy to find small concerns in our day and blow them out of proportion through fear, panic, or lack of trust in the One who beat even death. Jesus Christ has already faced our greatest fears and problems and removed the barrier. He has defeated death with His resurrection. We live in the certainty of knowing that because He lives, we too shall live. Our sins are forgiven through His perfect sacrificial death on the cross. He finds us trying to live between the rocks and the hard places of life, and He draws us back to Him through His heavenly gifts. He comes and frees us to truly live.

The stone has been rolled away. Christ is risen! He is risen indeed! Alleluia!

Returning Home

As a pastor, I've had plenty of close-up opportunities to see fathers hand over their daughters to soon-to-be husbands. There are those with trance-like stares and those who are visibly fidgety. And then there are those with last-minute words of love and advice that often bring tears to the daughter's eyes. To me, it is a very powerful moment when a father leads his daughter down the aisle, an important and emotional moment for the parents of both bride and groom. It marks the time when both woman and man leave their parents and are united. Good-byes can be difficult, but this is a unique farewell. This good-bye isn't permanent.

I have similar thoughts when considering Jesus' ascension—His good-bye. In considering Christ's good-bye and the marriage of the bridegroom, Jesus, and His bride, the Church, I keep coming back to my own family of origin.

Due to an accident at work, my father's soul ascended into heaven when he was about the same age as Jesus at His physical ascension. At the time my dad received new life in heaven, my mom was pregnant with me. My oldest brother, Don, was 12 years old. Almost 40 years later, Don wrote about a memory that reminds me of the disciples' joy in having Jesus around if only for a short time. Don allowed me to share part of this memory with you.

+ + + + +

It was after dark and Dad was still working outside. He was digging a hole or a ditch in the backyard where my swing set was or would be, I can't remember. I was running from tree to shed to bush playing some game of intrigue involving spies or cowboys, or maybe just enjoying being out after dark. And it really was pretty dark. No street or flood lights in this semi-rural setting. There was just the distant yellow light bulb on the back porch of our old farmhouse and the light from the kitchen window where Mom was doing the supper dishes.

It felt good knowing my dad was near, even if he was working. My play would carry me close to the hole now and then for the reassurance to venture out into the darkness again.

I sat at the lip of the hole and watched the shovel disappear into the dark shadow at the bottom, heard the "kachunk" as it sank into the gravelly dirt, and saw it reappear to deliver its load to the top of the nearby mound. As Dad came up with the loaded shovel, I could see in the dim light the white of his sleeveless undershirt and the beads of sweat on his strong, tight shoulders. I caught a whiff of his pungent, masculine odor. Some of the dirt rolled back down the mound and up against my legs, crossed in front me. Dad said, "Better get back, Donnie, before I have to dig you out." I got up to wander off again as he continued his smooth cycle of motions digging the hole.

He moved like that shovel was a part of him, or maybe he was part of it. Most memories of my dad include a tool of some kind. Dad worked. His job didn't pay what he was worth, so his only way to participate in the American Dream was to make improvements on those six acres and run-down old farmhouse. That is why, on this particular night, he was digging a ditch.

I ran over again and told him some childish riddle and made him guess at the answer. Without slowing his shovel, he smiled and made a few silly guesses, then made me tell him the answer. When I told him the not-too-funny punch line, he chuckled and said, "That's pretty good. Don't get too close there or you'll fall in."

I went off into the darkness. Dad was busy. He was different from Mom. He was a man who would support Mom and us kids and come around to fix things and make improvements. He would tousle our hair, share a meal, and be gone again. He was like the scout for a wagon train: respected, admired, well-liked, accepted as an important and integral part of the traveling family. He was the hero who went out and connected with, and protected the family from, the outside world. Yet by the very nature of his job, he was somehow set apart, distant, unknowable, mysterious, not really "in" as much as those who stayed in camp.

Dad straightened up, arched his back, and wiped some sweat from his eyebrow with his forearm. I came over and teasingly kicked a few clods of dirt back into the hole. He responded with mock anger, teasing that he ought to make me finish the digging. As he picked up the shovel and began his powerful down stroke, I said, "Okay!" and quickly jumped into the hole. I screamed in pain as the shovel hit my leg. I looked up and in the faint light I saw my dad's shocked face turn pale against the black sky. He bent down to examine the injury. He couldn't see in the darkness, but both of us could feel his fingers slipping over the blood on my leg. He scooped me into his arms and ran to the house, calling my mother's name. His voice was scared.

I closed my eyes against the stark, bright light of the kitchen. The image of the room and my mother moving toward us remained frozen in my brain while sounds told me everything was still in motion. Dad had me sitting on the kitchen table before the screen door had a chance to bang shut. Mom dabbed my leg with a damp cloth and it became clear that the wound was sizeable, but not deep. The shovel deflected off my shinbone and slid down my leg, scraping off skin as it went. I sobbed and dribbled tears as Mom applied first aid. Dad watched over her shoulder, went for scissors, helped hold gauze in place, and asked me how I was doing. With the worst of the crisis over, I thought he might get mad at me for jumping into the hole, but he never did. It was late and he decided to call it a night. He would leave the shovel outside and take a quick shower, and suggested we play a game of checkers or something.

A few minutes later he stood at the door to the living room with his hair still wet. As he walked toward me he asked, "How does it feel?" He sat down next to me on the couch and put his arm around me. His body was warm and damp from the shower. He smelled like Old Spice. I leaned into him and we just sat there. It felt so good. He was so tired he fell asleep in just a few minutes, but I didn't care. My dad, my hero, was in camp. And he loved me.

+ + + + +

Jesus came from the Father to pitch His tent among us, to camp with us. He loved being in camp with His disciples. He came to do His Father's work. He came because there was a crisis of sin: people needed to know of the Father's love and salvation. They needed to be healed of their sin, so the Father wrapped them with His forgiveness in Christ. He carried His children in His arms and brought them peace.

Although Jesus loved being in camp with His disciples, He belonged with His Father. He was preparing a place for all His disciples in heaven. And 40 days after His resurrection from the dead, He ascended. He returned home, but His presence would always be with His followers.

Snuggle up. God—Father, Daddy, Friend, Savior, your Hero—is in camp. And He loves you. And He leads us down the aisle to heaven.

Just as He Said

(Based on Matthew 28:6)

> The mood was somber; tears filled their eyes
> With Jesus' death their hope also dies.
> But women, wait! For death hasn't won,
> Stones nor death can hold God's own Son.
> Earthquake! An angel! An empty tomb!
> Then comes the news that shatters all gloom:
> The Son has risen in their mourning!
> Amidst their mourning, joy was roaring!
> Jesus, their Jesus, He is alive!
>
> He is alive! Just as He said!
> He conquered death! Just as He said!
> He lives for all! Just as He said!
> He gives us life! Just as He said!
>
> Our mood starts somber; sin fills our lives,
> But Easter news keeps our hope alive!
> Our Savior rose! That change brings us life—
> Hope reigns eternal amidst all strife.
> Heaven! Forgiveness! Abundant days!
> Abandon the fear—let's raise our praise!
> And trust the promises of our Lord
> As Easter blessings on us are poured!
> Jesus, our Jesus, He is alive!

He is alive! Just as He said!
  He conquered death! Just as He said!
  He lives for all! Just as He said!
  He gives us life! Just as He said!

A SEASON OF FAITH AND FIRE

& Five

Circle of Indemnity

One cold winter day in Denver, Colorado, while people were absorbed by the activities of life, a backdrop of snow and sleet fell to the ground. As the people of Denver went about their daily routines, one woman was focused solely on her child. Today was the day she was taking her newborn baby home from the hospital after a longer-than-usual stay. Shortly after birth, the child had open-heart surgery. Although the doctor probably didn't have to tell her, he reminded the new mom to be extra careful with the fragile child.

She buckled the newborn safely in the car seat, got in herself, locked the door, put on her seatbelt, and drove toward home. Icy rain and snow accumulated on the roads. She turned onto Interstate 25. The wind picked up, blowing the snow across the road, making it more difficult to see. She tightened her grip on the steering wheel and glanced in the back seat at her newborn. The windshield wipers moved in fast motion. Squinting and tense, she noticed something unusual ahead. A car had skidded out of control and was turned sideways. She was headed straight for it. She reacted quickly and slammed her foot on the brake. Her mind was on her frail, postoperative child as her car slid, heading right for the car in front of her. They slid down the interstate and stopped only inches from the other car. No impact whatsoever. Inches from a collision that could have been life threatening.

Before a sigh of relief could be released from her lungs, she noticed a semi-truck barreling down the highway and skidding right toward the two cars stuck in the traffic lane. She heard the brakes of the truck squeal as it jack-knifed and slid toward her car. The front of the truck stopped less than a foot from the hood of her car. And the back of the truck surrounded the other end. Again, no impact—at least for her vehicle carrying the frail baby. What occurred behind the truck was a 60-car pile-up. Cars crashed into the truck and into one another. It was one of the worst accidents the city had seen. But there, at the front of the heap was a car carrying a newborn baby recuperating from open-heart surgery.

As the media descended on the area, a reporter interviewed this mother. She told the reporter, "It was like I was in a circle of indemnity."

Her remark fascinated me. I pictured a crude-looking circle made by the jack-knifed truck and the car that surrounded her vehicle. But then I had to admit that although I was familiar with the word "indemnity," I wasn't positive of its meaning, so I looked it up in the dictionary. "Indemnity" refers to security against damage or loss. I couldn't get her story, words, or the visual picture out of my mind. A circle of indemnity. I love that idea and phrase. Since that story aired, I have referred to it many times in my life as I constantly find myself within the circle of indemnity God has created for me. Isn't that a wonderful picture? I love it!

Sometimes I think about it in connection with the great cloud of witnesses that surround me, as Hebrews 12:1–3 notes. Sometimes I visualize it regarding my Baptism—surrounded by family and Christian friends, pastors, sponsors, my church family, water, and God's Word.

And other times I picture myself standing safely in the middle of three great events: Jesus' crucifixion, His resurrection, and Pentecost. Swirling around each of these historical turning points for the world is the Wind—God, the Holy Spirit. (He is a warm Wind, not a harsh winter gust.)

I wonder if the disciples felt the way the lady in Denver did as she went from the hospital, through the storm, and then found herself in a circle of indemnity. They gathered with Jesus during Passover. They spent some time with Him praying, other times sleeping. Then came the horrible ordeal of His crucifixion, followed by the good news of His resurrection. After His ascension into heaven, they anxiously locked themselves in a room for fear of others storming in to harm them. But then came the Wind—the Holy Spirit. What was ahead?

At first it looked dangerous for them to openly proclaim the saving news to fellow Jews from all over the world that Jesus was truly the promised Savior of the world, their Messiah. But as the Spirit of God rested on them, they found safety. They were in a circle of indemnity. They boldly proclaimed the truth of Jesus, who died but then rose again and is the only way to heaven. What security and confidence they had because of that circle of indemnity. The Holy Spirit used that situation on the day of Pentecost to bring at least 3000 people within His "circle of security against damage or loss" through Baptism.

God continues to provide His circle of indemnity. He uses His promises as well as His presence. Through His faithfulness, He creates a circle of indemnity. He may use a gentle whisper or His Spirit's mighty power. He uses a small piece of bread and a sip of wine and uses the waters of Baptism. The Lord Himself is a circle of indemnity, our refuge and strong fortress, and He carries us into the circle safely on wings like eagles.

If you have hit a patch of ice in your life, know that the Lord brings you to safety within His circle of indemnity. If your journey seems safe and secure, give thanks for His circle of safety that surrounds you. Rest securely, confidently, as He lovingly steers you into His circle of salvation.

From *The Message*

... The moment we get tired in the waiting,
God's Spirit is right alongside helping us along. If
we don't know how or what to pray, it doesn't
matter. He does our praying in and for us, making
prayer out of our wordless sighs, our aching
groans. He knows us far better than we know our-
selves ... and keeps us present before God. That's
why we can be so sure that every detail in our lives
of love for God is worked into something good.

(adapted from Romans 8:26–28)

FROM MY THOUGHTS

Holy Spirit,

Take my wordless sighs and aching groans.
Shape them into the perfect prayer—which is one
in accordance to the will of my Savior. Present
them to the Father in Jesus' name. The sighs and
groans are Yours now. I shall rest securely, trust
completely, and wait patiently for the Father's perfect answer.

The Weeping Tree

By no means am I an expert on growing fruit trees. And my son must follow in my steps. I learned this when he was just a few years old. My wife bought an apple tree. We dug the hole, added fertilizer, planted the tree, and drenched it with water. My son wanted to call his grandparents to tell them about this, his latest adventure. He told his grandfather, "Pop-pop, we just planted an apple tree and now we're going to put apples on it!" As I said, I'm no expert. But I know that's not how it works.

I also know about living the Spirit-filled life that produces the fruit of the Holy Spirit. I know about it because the Bible tells me so. Jesus told His disciples, "I am the Vine, you are the branches. If a man remains in Me and I in him, he will bear much fruit; apart from Me you can do nothing" (John 15:5). And I recently found out a little more about fruit bearing—growing apples and producing fruit of the Spirit.

A young man at a conference told a group of teens about his father, who went to an orchard and bought 25 apple trees. The family was excited when, four years later, the trees began producing fruit. His father loved caring for the trees and picking the apples. For a dozen years, all of the trees except one were bearing fruit. One summer his father decided to ask an orchard farmer about this particular tree. The farmer knew what was wrong. He said it had never been wounded. He went on to explain that orchard workers make sure to nick or scrape trees until they "weep"—until sap runs from them. Apple trees need to be wounded and weep before they can produce fruit.

The man went home and drove a 16-penny nail into his barren tree until it wept. The next year that one tree bore more fruit than all the others combined! It had 12 years of fruit-bearing potential in it, but its potential had been locked inside.

You know what I'm going to write, don't you? How much potential does God see in you? God only knows—literally. We all know people who don't want to be wounded so they won't have to weep. I think deep down we all know, but don't always want to admit, that God does amazing things through pain, grief, and struggles. Being wounded is never easy. For apple trees to bear fruit, being wounded is necessary. That doesn't have to be the case for humans, but God knows the potential that lies behind the wounds. And through His own wounds, received upon the ultimate "weeping tree," His children bear fruit.

I realize that some will view this as a sappy story. (I'm sorry. I just couldn't resist the pun!) Many people don't want to read about being wounded or especially about weeping. For others, I pray, you are reading this at a time when you are ready to, needing to, or in the middle of a good cry. If you are experiencing pain as great as having a nail driven through your body, Jesus can relate. He's been there. He knows pain. He knows what weeping is all about. He's been there too. And through the pain of nails driven through His body, He bore life-giving fruit—forgiveness, hope, and salvation.

How much potential fruit is in you? Only God knows if you are weeping or ready to weep. Allow Him to take your wounded heart and cause your life to overflow with His life-giving fruit—fruit that will last.

Standing under His Understanding

I can't count the number of times I've said it. Most times it just slips out. I've said it at funeral homes, in hospital rooms, in counseling sessions, and even in conversations with strangers. There are times it just seems like the right thing to say. Most of the time I say it to comfort others, but I don't know how often I succeed. I would guess you are familiar with the phrase because you've said it and you've heard it.

"I understand what you're going through."

Those are the familiar words. On one hand, if someone is going through a difficult time, it can be comforting to know others relate to the situation. It can be very helpful to talk to someone who has walked across a similar high wire and made it safely to the other side.

On the other hand, those words of understanding bring little or no comfort because the person speaking the words cannot really understand. Every situation is different, emotions are diverse, and often no one can completely understand what is happening in someone else's heart and life.

But I hope you understand that one thing is certain ... there is One who truly understands. Not only that, He knows you better than you know yourself. He has searched even your subconscious thoughts. Before a word is on your tongue, He knows it completely. Trust Him, He understands.

If you're not convinced that Jesus knows how it feels to wrestle with something that needs to be done, sit with Him on Maundy Thursday. Watch and listen. Look at Him struggling with His Father and His emotions. Wipe the sweat that seems like drops of blood forming on His forehead.

If you think Jesus couldn't possibly understand your feelings of lowliness at living below the poverty level ... think again. This is the King of kings, who was born in a manure-filled stable.

Maybe you're not sure Jesus understands how it feels to have a job that is degrading or work that is unpleasant. If so, you'll have to wait in that line over there behind the disciples. When it's your turn, you can tell Jesus He doesn't understand while He washes your feet.

You can tell Jesus that He doesn't understand the pain and emotions of a divorce right after Judas kisses Him in the Garden of Gethsemane.

If you don't think Jesus can sympathize with your difficulty in dealing with a rift in your family, remember that His own brothers rejected Him and His claim to be Savior.

How can Jesus understand the temptation you are struggling with in doing something purely for your own advancement? Stand with Him on the mountaintop. Join Him in looking Satan in the eyes while he devilishly tries to trip Him up.

You think He doesn't understand the pain of separation death has caused? Take a handkerchief when you join Him outside Lazarus's tomb. You can use it to wipe His tears while He wipes away yours.

Feeling rejected? How could Jesus understand? Spend time with Him tonight and read John 1:11 ... "He came to that which was His own, but His own did not receive Him."

Wondering if Jesus could conceive of the frustration you have being surrounded by apathy and indifference? Maybe you should help Him wake His sleeping disciples when He asks them to watch and pray.

"I feel like I'm being pulled in 23 directions!" Do you doubt that Jesus ever cried those words to His Father? Tag along as thousands want to hear His every word; the sick beg for His touch; the disciples need His attention and teaching; the Pharisees test His words and nerves; the officials call for His head; and His own body craves rest and prayer.

How can this Jesus, who has people flocking all around Him, understand what it's like to be lonely? Consider the 40 days spent alone in the wilderness. Or maybe you'd like to discuss it with Him while He's on the cross. (Wait, He's saying something ... "My God, My God, why have You forsaken Me?") He understands.

Dealing with physical pain? Can't you hear the soldiers pounding the nails through His flesh? Are people making fun of you? Listen to the cries, "Crucify Him! Crucify Him!" that still echo throughout the land.

"The prognosis isn't good, Lord. No one is talking about it, but I know I'm dying. They know I'm dying. I've never felt emotions like this, Lord. Have You, Lord?" Join Him at Calvary. Hear Him say, "It is finished." What that means is that your prognosis is getting better—perfectly better—in a little while.

You see, Jesus is the only One who *can* say, "I understand how you feel," and mean it. Mix that truth with His heart of compassion and His knowledge of how to best meet your needs. Stand at the foot of His cross. Hear His words and dine at His table. And receive His comfort that surpasses all your needs.

So the next time you need some understanding (which is probably this very moment), stand under His understanding.

+ + + + +

"Nothing in all creation is hidden in God's sight. Everything is uncovered and laid bare before the eyes of Him to whom we must give account. Therefore, since we have a great high Priest who has gone through the heavens, Jesus the Son of God, let us hold firmly to the faith we profess. For we do not have a high Priest who is unable to sympathize with our weaknesses, but we have one who has been tempted *in every way, just as we are*—yet was without sin. Let us then approach the throne of grace with confidence, so that we may receive mercy and *find grace to help us in our time of need*." (Hebrews 4:13–16. Italics added for emphasis.)

Just Passing By (Almost)

Why do they make the squares on calendars so small? Some days it's difficult to squeeze our packed schedule into a 24-hour period let alone into one of those little squares. Most lives are bursting with overcrowded, out-of-control schedules. You're familiar with the schedule you battle each week. Let me give you another sample of an inspiring journal/calendar account I found recently:

- Trip home—doesn't look promising;
- Teaching schedule—increase to full-time;
- Plan, prepare, and send co-workers on out-of-town trips;
- Co-workers return—debriefing limited, schedule too crowded;
- Death and funeral of relative;
- No time to eat—meals canceled;
- Quiet, restful time postponed;
- Conduct outdoor lecture for over-flow crowd;
- Prepare meal for thousands;
- After lecture, friends take off in boat for a break;
- Private prayer vigil in mountains until three a.m.;
- Take a walk;
- Pass by friends in boat—almost.

That's a busy schedule to say the least. Maybe you can relate to some of the entries. If you want to read more about them, look in the Bible. Mark 6 will walk you through a short span of Jesus' ministry on earth. If you are familiar with God's Word, you may be acquainted with the stops along Jesus' path as Mark recorded: Jesus' trip home without honor; Jesus sends out the disciples; John the Baptizer beheaded; Jesus feeds more than five thousand, followed by time alone in prayer; the disciples head out on the sea in a boat; Jesus walks on the water and was about to pass the disciples by ...

Wait a minute! Jesus was walking on the water and was about to pass them by? There are seven words in Mark's gospel that share that fact. They are easy words to pass by. (There's a great difference in Jesus almost passing by 12 of His disciples and our passing by seven words in Scripture.)

Jesus knew the disciples were in the boat. In fact, the Bible tells us He saw them straining at the oars because the wind was against them. It was the middle of the night— three or four o'clock in the morning. His week had been filled with storm-like experiences. People were straining for His attention. The wind of God's Spirit was blowing through His words. Although His teaching schedule was packed, Jesus took time to teach the disciples in the middle of the night, in the middle of a lake, in the middle of a storm. He couldn't just pass up the opportunity. And so He went walking on the lake. He was about to pass them by when the disciples cried out to Him in fear.

Jesus responded to their cries. Immediately He said to them, "Take courage! It is I. Don't be afraid." Then He climbed into the boat with them, and the wind died down (Mark 6:50b–51).

Class dismissed. Did the lesson just pass you by? I think the lesson planned for the floating classroom could be simply titled: Emergency 101. The professor was Jesus, the Master Teacher. The course syllabus included "Courage in Desperate Times," "For Crying out Loud," and "The Calming Affect of Jesus." The graduation song was "Call on Me."

Be still. Right now, be still. Is Jesus trying to get your attention? Will you pass Him by because you don't see Him? Is the One who walks on water asking you not to walk past the help and calming gifts He has for you? Maybe you're missing the Teacher or His lesson because your focus is on the storm or on your boat as you strain to keep afloat.

He sees you straining at the oars, trying to get through the winds of temptation; your stormy relationships; your job, or lack of one, that is blowing you off course; or whatever is causing you fear, worry, or sadness. Jesus Christ calms the storm. So why are you waiting? Cry out! Call to Him! He wants you to call on Him instead of fighting the storm by yourself. As you call out to Him, Jesus immediately will say to you, one of His disciples, "Take courage! It is I. Don't be afraid."

If your week is cluttered or your schedule is overcrowded or even if you're stuck in a rut of mundane routine, Jesus doesn't want you to pass Him by. He has promised to never leave you or forsake you. He comes to you in the water. He comes to you in His Word. He comes to you in the bread and wine. As you strain on the oars, strain your eyes to see the water-walking Savior. Gladly, Jesus climbs into your "life boat" and gives you courage for the ride as He brings a calming peace to the storms of your cluttered life. What a perfect place to anchor!

I Want Off This Roller Coaster!

Call me a wimp, a chicken—whatever you'd like. But plain and simple, I don't like roller coasters! I think it has to do with things like nausea, dizziness, and the feeling that I'm going to go flying off into the air without a padded cushion to land on! But about every decade of my life I take a dumb-and-dumber pill and climb back into the seat, strap down, and try it again. I think, *surely I'll be okay this time*. But the results are the same. By the time I'm flying down the first drop, I know it was a mistake. *What was I thinking?* While everyone else is screaming from fun, I'm screaming, "I want off this roller coaster!" And this may be a shock to you, but not once has an amusement park employee actually stopped a control coaster and let me off in the middle of the ride. Where is their compassion, I ask?

I remember one particular roller coaster ride I was on with a friend. I found out during the ride that she didn't like roller coasters either. In fact, in the middle of the ride she handed me a note that read, "I want off this roller coaster!" I learned that some of the reasons for her dislike of this roller coaster were the same as mine: nausea, dizziness, and fear of flying off with no safe landing in sight. However, she had additional reasons for wanting off the roller coaster.

The day she handed me the note, we were sitting next to each other on the ride. We weren't strapped in though. And we weren't at an amusement park. In fact, there was nothing amusing about her situation or the note. We were sitting next to each other—on her sofa. My friend, Laurie, handed me her thoughts on paper because she was unable to speak at the time. Laurie was battling cancer of the throat and tongue. At one point, three-fourths of her tongue was removed. During that surgery, a part of the muscle in her forearm was removed, reshaped, and attached to what was left of the muscle in her mouth to create a new tongue for her. Sometime later, the cancer spread into the new muscle and her entire tongue was removed.

This is just a little part of what she went through. There was chemotherapy, multiple surgeries, cancer seemingly moving to her lungs, exhausting trips to doctors' offices and hospitals, and so on. On top of it all, Laurie, a single mother, was striving to raise her three-year-old son, Zach.

Laurie was weak and worn out, not just from all the difficulties she faced but because amidst all the suffering would come news that brought her hope. Then bad news. Good news. Tough news. Hopeful news. Feeling weak. Feeling somewhat strong.

It was like a roller coaster. Things are coasting along okay. A little hill to climb. Not bad. Hey, nice vieeeeeeeewwwwww! Then comes the downhill spiral. Corkscrews. Twisting, hanging upside down, and zooming in every direction at amazing speeds. There is the calm … for a short while. Close your eyes and hold on for dear life! Stomach drops. Dizziness. Fear. Nausea. I want off this roller coaster!

You don't have to fight the horrors of cancer to know what it feels like to be on an emotional, mental, or spiritual roller coaster. I would imagine we've all ridden one—mostly against our will.

I remember staring at Laurie's words on the paper, "I want off this roller coaster!" Who was I to argue with that? In my wildest imagination, I couldn't comprehend what she was going through. I would want off too. What could I say that would bring her comfort? I stared at the paper for about thirty seconds, unable to look her in the eye because I didn't have a response. Then the Holy Spirit gave me the words. They came to my mind faster than any roller coaster.

I took her hand and looked her in the eye and let the Spirit talk through me. "Laurie," I said, "I don't like roller coasters either. I detest them in fact. But I think I just realized why I feel that way. Roller coasters give you the impression that you are not in control ... and, in truth, you're not! Roller coasters take you places in ways you've never been before. That's scary in itself. But at the same time, they give you the illusion that you are going to go flying off an uncontrollable monster. But that's not true. In fact, there is something you can't see while you're riding it. It's hidden under the cars. It's a beam attached securely to each section of the ride. It's there to keep you on track, so you cannot fly off.

"You wrote that you wanted off this roller coaster. That makes all the sense in the world. You receive good news followed by bad; you feel strong then weak. The roller coaster isn't fun. But what I can tell you is that although it may feel like God is nowhere in sight, He *is* in control. You can't see the big picture—no one can. But He has you in His grip. He is holding on to you. Like the beams under roller coasters, God is in control. There is nothing wrong with wanting off, but if you want off because you think God doesn't care or isn't in control, then you need to ask God to give you a new perspective. Ask Him to help you take a look at the superstructure of the ride. If you look at a roller coaster from the ground up, you see the beam that keeps the ride on track. Instead of riding the roller coaster every day, allow yourself to just look from the ground. There you can see the security of how the ride was made.

"In the same way, Laurie, stand on the ground on which you have been raised—and raise your eyes to the cross. From that vantage point, you can see God's promises and know He is in control. Jesus is the beam that keeps you from flying off and crashing. He promises to never let go of you."

The visit ended in prayer, a long silence, and tears.

I know the roller coasters we experience as we live in a sinful world aren't fun. But when we take a different perspective—from the ground looking up—we see that we are in God's eternal grip of love and He is in control, no matter what ups and downs our lives take.

What's on Your Mantel and under Your Mantle?

What's on your mantel? Or what would you put on it if you had one? I think you can learn something about people from what they put on their mantelpiece—framed photographs, a diploma, candles, books, or maybe a plaque inscribed with a Bible verse.

It's fun to guess what the objects on a mantel tell about people—but those items tell a limited story. Pictures can tell how many people are in a family and how nicely each of them can smile. But a photograph on a mantel tells nothing about the relationships behind the smiles. Mantels can showcase a degree from a prestigious college or seminary, yet if there is no godly degree of faith, love, compassion, and forgiveness, an education means little. You might guess a person is a Christian if they display a Scripture verse on their mantel. But if God's Word is not written on his or her heart, that changes everything.

The items on our mantel do not tell that particular story. To find out about a person's faith walk with Jesus, you have to look somewhere else. You will find that greater story *under* a person's *mantle*.

Notice that's m-a-n-t-l-e. The piece over a fireplace is m-a-n-t-e-l. Note the spelling difference. If you don't know the definition for this other word, turn to 1 Kings 19 in the King James Version of the Bible. This is the story where God calls Elisha into ministry and uses a worn out and dejected prophet named Elijah to be His calling vessel.

Remember Elijah's story? He was on the run for his life. The Lord strengthened him and told him to go to the mountain of God. On the mountain, the Lord spoke to Elijah—not through an earthquake, fire, or great wind, but through a gentle whisper. God directed Elijah to go to Elisha, who would succeed him as prophet. So Elijah went from there and found Elisha, son of Shaphat. He was plowing with 12 yoke of oxen. "... Elijah passed by him, and cast his mantle upon him" (1 Kings 19:19b KJV).

God called Elisha to be His prophet, and the calling process included a mantle—Elijah's cloak—around him as one set apart by God. Elijah's mantle told others a lot about him. It told the world that He was a prophet of God. That's why Elisha knew immediately what it meant when Elijah placed his mantle on him.

Although Elijah didn't know much about his successor, God knew everything about him. God not only knew what Elisha had on his mantel, in his house over his fireplace, He also knew what Elisha had under his mantle, the prophet's cloak. God knew about the picture of faith beautifully framed in Elisha's heart. He was well aware of Elisha's degrees of trust, love, and compassion for the lost. And God's Word was written on His heart, not on a plaque on his fireplace mantel.

God cares about every aspect of our lives, but His first concern is what we have under our mantle regarding our calling to be His dearly loved children. Look at Jesus' three-year ministry on earth. While He ministered to people's physical hurts, His utmost concern was their faith. Then consider the day that Jesus' mantle, His cloak, was stripped from Him as the soldiers threw dice for it. Jesus hung on what could have been used as a fireplace mantel, a piece of timber. But under that rugged wood, a fire of love for the world roared. Its flames can never be put out.

As we come to the cross, the Breath of God ignites a roaring fire of faith within us. It is kindled daily through His Word and Baptism. He fans the flame with His body and blood, offering forgiveness. And the Breath of God burns with an urgency to share His message of peace with the world. It brings light to every dark place in the world, melting hearts frozen with bitterness and pain.

So what is on your mantel and under your mantle? God has an eternally sturdy, life-changing "mantel-*peace*" to cover every aspect of your life.

Give Thanks for What?

Wouldn't it be nice if we put more emphasis on giving thanks throughout the year and not just on Thanksgiving Day? Giving thanks is easy, isn't it? Well, most of the time it's easy. But what about those things for which we don't want to be thankful? What about the tough times?

Many churches use the story of the 10 lepers healed by Jesus for a Thanksgiving reading. Consider the lepers. They were shut off from their families and communities and lived as outcasts. They had a terrible illness that brought constant pain. Grief was a part of their lives as they dealt with the loss of friends, family, and even parts of their bodies. And what about the loneliness, sadness, despair, depression, and fear they must have struggled with because of their burden of leprosy?

For fun (and for a faith lesson), let's take on the role of one of those lepers—the only one who returned thanks to Jesus after he was healed of his life-threatening disease.

The Bible tells us that he came back praising Jesus and thanking Him. It doesn't say exactly what the man said to Him, although it seems obvious that he would have given thanks for healing. But let's take it a step further. I wonder if sometime later—days, months, or even years—the healed man realized that if it weren't for the leprosy, he wouldn't have become a believer. Did he realize that if he hadn't been afflicted with the sickening disease, he likely wouldn't have met his Healer at all? Or consider how much better he must have been, how compassionate, following his healing, in ministering to others and to their families. Maybe his family didn't know about Jesus and they came to faith after his healing.

Who knows? God may have used what seemed to be nothing but a horrible situation to change the daily and eternal lives of many people.

Giving thanks is easy, isn't it? Well, most of the time it's easy. But do we give thanks even when surrounded by pain, illness, heartaches, or other problems? I know I often forget. It's easy to give thanks when things go smoothly. But aren't we to be thankful to God in *all* things?

When praying for someone battling a terminal illness, I often wonder how God may be using the situation to strengthen the faith of someone nearby. How often does God use a death to bring new life to others or cause them to reexamine His eternal plan? Even when a child dies, we can thank the heavenly Father for the gift of eternal life for that child, wrapped in grace.

Perhaps God used the loss of a job to open the door to another opportunity where you could better serve Him. Don't forget that He knows what is best for you and wants His best for you.

Remember when someone intended to hurt you and God used it for good? What about the break-up of a relationship you thought was right? Or the pregnancy you wanted but wasn't to be?

Our ways are not God's ways. But His grace is sufficient for us. He promises to work for the good of all those who love Him. And He gives your eyes of faith new vision to see how He can take a horrible experience and turn it into a gift to be used for His glory.

"Jesus, Master, have mercy on me!" Is it time for that cry to come from our hearts and lips? Cry out to the Master and listen as He calls you by name and responds with a heart of compassion. Receive His cleansing gift of forgiveness. Stand in awe as He works miracles in your life. He may not always lead in the direction you expect, but you can rely on His promise that He works for your good.

I guess we won't know more about the healed leper's life and faith this side of heaven. But our faith continues to grow as we learn more about the life and love of our Savior, Jesus. And we have plenty to give thanks for as we place our lives—all aspects of our lives—into His hands.

Give thanks in all circumstances!

Make Me Brand New

Why do I put the cross at arm's length
  When Jesus went to such great lengths to save me?
  Why am I blind to those with great needs
  When Jesus gave me sight and all that I need?
  Why am I such a stumbling block
  To God's faithful chosen who live on the Rock?

Change me. Forgive me. Make me brand new.
  Wash me. Absolve me. I'll follow You.
  Jesus, redeem me. Make me brand new.
  Spirit, renew me. Make my heart true.

It's time to run to Calvary's cross—
  There to find hope and forgiveness in Jesus.
  Why He died for me boggles my mind,
  But my Spirit-created faith says thank You.
  Why I cling to the cross of Christ now
  Is because He changed me. Christ made me brand
  new.

Change me. Forgive me. Make me brand new.
  Wash me. Absolve me. I'll follow You.
  Jesus, redeem me. Make me brand new.
  Spirit, renew me. Make my heart true.

Robert

I turned to the last page of the letter and read the closing words, "I am not proud of where I am or what I did to get here. I was forced to come to grips with reality a long time ago. I know what is in store for me in my future. Death comes to us all at one time or another, I simply know how mine will come."

The letter writer had a unique perspective. Most people cannot say they know what is in store for their future or how their death will come. Although it would seem the person who wrote these words was very near death, he lived seven years after he wrote that letter to me.

He lived in a small community about an hour and a half away. And I will never forget our friendship, the impact He had on my life, or that we shared the God of grace.

Although he hadn't attended in years, the letter writer, Robert, was a member of the church I served as pastor. We stayed in contact by letter and phone, as well as personal visits. Robert always made the phone calls. I always made the drive so we could visit. We shared the letter writing.

I was the first one to make contact with Robert, by mail. I introduced myself as his new pastor and wondered how I could best minister to him, offering my compassion and friendship, along with an ear to listen. His first letter, from which I already quoted, also included this proposal: "I can offer you three things without hesitation: friendship, honesty, and information. All you need do is ask and I shall tell you what you want to know. Be advised, the truth is not always pretty."

Ugly truth and all, I took that as an open invitation. I looked forward to meeting Robert in person, but it took some doing. There were requests to be made, people to contact, as well as papers to copy in triplicate and place on file. Even pastors can't just show up at the door and expect to see a death row inmate in a maximum-security prison.

Robert had called this facility home for three or four years. Our first meeting was held behind glass. After some chitchat and getting to know each other, Robert asked if I knew what he had done. Although I had talked to his family about coming to see him, they had not shared the story that had led to his home on death row. I wondered if what I was about to hear was "the truth that wasn't always pretty."

With humility and sadness, he recounted the events that had brought him to this place filled with guards, bare walls, and myriad security devices. Before he began, Robert told me he accepted what he had coming to him—death by lethal injection. He had done something terribly wrong. My new friend was sorry for his actions.

Robert was in college when he got involved in drugs. He was strung out for three straight weeks when he got word of someone else's drug deal gone bad. He was irate. He stopped his dialogue to tell me that he didn't use the drugs as an excuse, but he was certain there was no way he would have done this if it weren't for the drugs. Robert then told me of his plan to get back at this dealer over a $100 deal. He sought out the dealer and made her drive to a wooded area. There he tied her up in the car, set it on fire, and shot her two times in the back.

Time seemed to stand still. I remember looking him in the eye throughout every detail. This seemed so foreign to my life, yet one fact jumped out in front of my face. It wasn't the drugs, the kidnapping, the fire, or the shooting. Well, it was all of those things in one sense. But in another it wasn't any of them that stood out with prominence. It was this thought that kept running through my mind: "We have a God who can forgive even this." I couldn't get that truth out of my head or heart. Yes, Robert's story is horrific—but at the same time, the flip side of the story taught me more about the incredible gift of God's forgiveness.

Daily I would travel to the cross of Jesus Christ, but this trip was different. The Lord wanted Robert to come along. He was hurting. At one time in his life, Robert knew about the hill called Golgotha outside the city limits of Jerusalem where His Savior, Jesus, was crucified. But it had been some time since Robert had gone there and he seemed to have lost direction. He felt he was locked inside the city gates and he'd never reach the cross or even recognize Jesus if he could get close enough.

What Robert didn't realize is that Jesus holds in His hand the key to free any person locked in any prison of sin and guilt. He didn't seem to remember that Jesus would seek him out. And there was no doubt that Jesus would recognize him. Robert's face, heart, and life were etched in Jesus' heart. Jesus knew Robert before the beginning of the world and before the beginning of the day we met with a partition of glass between us and prison guards around us.

As I shared this news, reminding and assuring my repentant brother of the forgiveness Jesus offers, it was as though I could hear the gate being unlocked and Robert walking out, free of chains. Together we headed straight for the cross. We arrived just in time to hear a fellow prisoner speak. "Jesus, remember me when You come into Your kingdom." Jesus told the criminal, "I tell you the truth, today you will be with Me in paradise" (Luke 23:42–43).

Robert had been charged with kidnapping and murder. It was as if the Savior of the world was now facing Robert. And at that moment, it was Jesus who was guilty of stealing. Jesus stole Robert's heart. Jesus took the chains of sin that entangled Robert and He destroyed them. Our Lord stole Robert's old life and offered him a new one.

Being an eyewitness to it all made me realize something else. Jesus was also changing me.

Robert's case came up for appeal several times through the years. There were always delays. Along the way our relationship continued. Sometimes we would talk or write weekly and sometimes months would pass. I sent Robert a Bible and led some "Bible-studies-by-mail" with him. I loved to read about his insights into God's Word. He also had his struggles. It was difficult to lead a Christian life on death row. Life in prison was filled with revenge, jealousy, deceit, and false information. Sometimes it was extremely difficult for him to deal with that day-to-day environment and the intricate scheming that goes with it.

Robert had a particular concern about his execution that he would bring out in conversation from time to time. With an execution came publicity. He didn't want that. He had put his family through so much already, he didn't want to cause them more pain. Robert didn't know how to handle that aspect of his walk to death.

Over time, God's Spirit seemed to rest on my imprisoned, yet freed, friend. He started and participated in Bible study groups and support groups for the families of prisoners, and he found ways to care for prisoners' children. He became very active in living.

Then came the notification. There were no more appeals. The final date for his execution was set.

He didn't tell me of the news.

The telephone rang at 10:05 p.m. It wasn't a collect call—the only kind Robert could make from prison. Rather, it was a local call. The phone lines were filled with wailing. Between the tearful gasps, I recognized the voice. It was Robert's mom. She said she had just received a call from the prison. Robert was dead.

It wasn't a lethal injection that killed him. Earlier that December day Robert had attended a Bible class. His deepest desire was to do what was best for his family so they wouldn't have to go through his execution and all it involved. So, using extension cords, he hung himself in his cell.

His family asked me to have his funeral service. After his mom and I shared stories and time together that night, I spent the next day in my office crying while reading all of the letters Robert had sent me.

I walked into the funeral home for the service, asking the Holy Spirit to rest on me and give me the words to speak that would bring comfort to his family. I expected to be sharing God's Word and thoughts with only Robert's family, maybe 10 people at the most. So you can imagine my shock when I walked into the room and found it over-flowing with people. I had no idea who they were.

God's Spirit held me up and followed through on His promise to give me the words. Although I knew of Robert's faith and his forgiven life, I especially struggled with his suicide. Robert, who was facing death by lethal injection, had done it for the sake of his family—and yet it was a sin, it was wrong. I also knew that when Jesus died on the cross, His forgiveness and perfection covered the past, present, and future sins of all those who live and die believing in Him. There was also my concern that if I spoke only of Robert being in heaven because of the grace of Jesus and the Spirit-created faith of my friend, I could be giving others in the room "permission" to commit sui-cide. After much prayer, the words flowed and I felt confident that the Spirit was speaking in the language of those who needed to hear. I can't remember what exactly I said, but I know God's Spirit led me.

After the service, I moved to the back of the room to let people greet the family. God didn't stop there in open-ing His heart of grace. After greeting the family, the other mourners lined up to speak to me. Along with their hugs, I received words like, "Thank you so much. My son is on death row. ... My husband is in for life. Thank you for the hope you shared. ... My brother appreciated all Robert did, and I appreciate how God used you today." I especially remember one large man who gave me a bear hug while speaking into my ear. "My son was just transferred to a prison in Indiana. He's in for life. He doesn't know Jesus Christ. Will you pray for him? Pray that the Lord will use someone like you to bring Jesus to him. Please pray for him." I assured him I would.

As people left the funeral, I was filled with a mixture of emotions. I felt sad and a bit lonely. But I also felt hopeful and used by God. Confusion and wonderment combined for a unique mix in my mind and heart. I was curious about the effect of God's Word on the people in that room and their imprisoned relatives and friends. I also felt the comfort of Jesus' arms around me. He would be the one to judge Robert's life, death, and faith, but I would hold on, with hope, that I would see Robert again one day.

I will never forget our relationship, the impact he had on my life, or the God of grace we share.

Epilogue

I know the effect God's Word and its revelation of my Savior, Jesus Christ, has had on me. I was born, like you, like Robert, with a death sentence. But the God of grace, whom we share by faith, has exchanged the mandate of death for a life sentence through His life, death, and resurrection. I knew that fact before I met Robert or heard about T. J., Tony, Lorna, Kendall, and Mario. I loved that truth before I ministered to my friends in the nursing home or read about the woman with a twisted mouth and her husband with a twisted love. I trusted the life-giving facts of Jesus before I truly understood the power of the Holy Spirit on Pentecost or found a mother and child safe within a circle of indemnity. But as God worked through Robert and all the rest, I know love and trust in the life-saving, sin-forgiving gift of Jesus Christ in a more powerful way. They have helped me to always be prepared to witness to His faithfulness to us. I pray they have helped prepare you until we meet, by grace, in the season of heaven; the season that has no end.

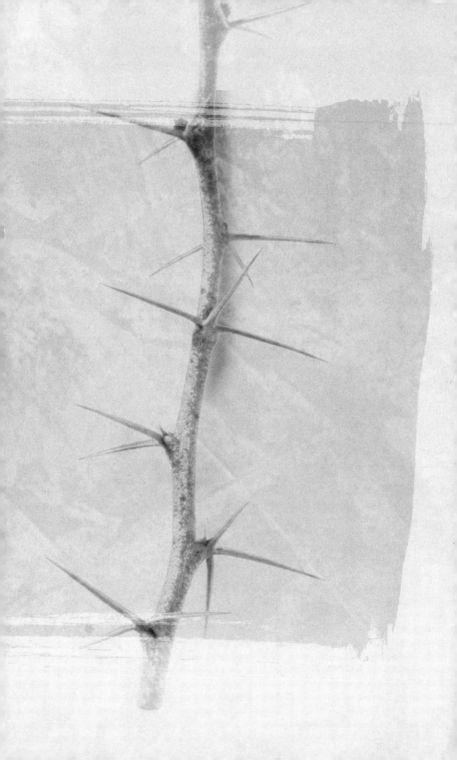